D1593215

EDMUND WALLER

POEMS
1645

Together with

Poems from Bodleian MS Don D 55

SCOLAR PRESS 1971

Printed in Great Britain by
The Scolar Press Limited
Menston, Yorkshire, England

NOTE

Reproduced (original size) from a copy in the Bodleian Library, by permission of the Curators. Shelf-mark: Don f 144.

Edmund Waller (1606-1687) was deeply involved in the political life of his times. Although a moderate supporter of reform in 1640, in 1643 he was arrested by parliament for plotting with the king. He went into exile in 1645, and yet was allowed to return only ten years later. These waverings in his political position are clearly reflected in his poetry: he wrote eulogies on both Charles I and Cromwell.

His political activities had a direct effect on the text of the poems reproduced here, for in 1645, when they first appeared in print, Waller was an exile in Paris, and played no part in the publication of the first two editions of that year. No doubt his poems had circulated privately in manuscript for some time before this date, as, for example, Donne's did long before the publication of the *Poems* of 1633, but as a gentleman-poet with court connections, it is unlikely that Waller ever considered publication. Clearly, however, one of these manuscripts came into the hands of the bookseller Thomas Walkley, who caused it to be printed. Since he did not enter his book in the *Stationers' Register*, we cannot be certain that he owned the copy, but the form of words on the title-page of the first issue of the first edition (Wing W 511) suggests that he did. Shortly after publication, he seems to have sold his rights in the copy to Humphrey Mosley, who published all subsequent editions with which we are concerned here.

Three editions were published by Mosley in 1645. To begin with, he re-issued the first edition with a new title-page. The title-page of the Walkley issue has an ornamental border, and in some copies, the words '*Imprimatur* Na. Brent. *Decem.* 30. 1644.' (The British Museum has copies with and without the imprimatur – C. 57. k. 21. and C. 57. k. 22.) The Mosley issue has a plain typographical title-page and no imprimatur; the wording of this title-page is exactly the same as that of the edition reproduced here. Wing does not distinguish between these two issues, but facsimiles are printed by Chew (see below). In addition to the poems, the first edition also contains some of Waller's speeches. The second edition is a reprint, without the speeches of the first (Wing W 512); it is reproduced here because the Bodleian copy has certain interesting features which are discussed below. The third edition (Wing W 513) is a further reprint, although with corrections apparently made from a holograph manuscript; Chew states that there is a fine paper issue of this edition. In this edition the speeches are restored.

Signatures A and I (the final signature of *Poems*) were originally printed on the same sheet and in the Bodleian copy reproduced here they have not been separated by the binder; the order of the leaves of the first gathering is A 1 (title-page), I 2, I 1, A 2, A 3, I 4, I 3, A 4. In the following facsimile these leaves have been placed in the correct order.

Don f 144, in addition to the poems, contains two other items of great interest, which probably alter Chew's conclusions about the order of the editions and issues of 1645:

(a) three of Waller's speeches to the House of Commons, including his defence of himself to the House after his arrest. These are in fact sheets of the third edition, but the next item, and the binding, suggest that this copy at least, and possibly others, were issued with these sheets as an integral part of the book;

(b) a list of books in print published and sold by Mosley, including poems by Donne, Carew, Davenant and others, and many plays. Item no. 83 in this list is '*Poems*, &c. written by *Mr. Edward* [sic] *Waller* of *Beconsfield,* Esq. 8°', which seems to suggest that this list was compiled after the publication of Mosley's issue of Wing W 511, i.e. the first edition. This list is clearly an item which Mosley would wish to distribute as widely as possible, and he may be supposed to have included it in every book which he sold after it was printed, which was presumably at some time during 1645.

That this list is preserved here argues that the first owner of the volume (Don f 144) – presumably Bridget Heveningham, sister of the regicide William Heveningham, whose autograph appears on the title-page in a contemporary hand – carefully preserved the whole of the material which she acquired when she bought Waller's poems. The argument is strengthened by the fact that the binding is almost certainly contemporary with publication, and may have been made for the owner immediately after the book was first bought. This suggests that the speeches, despite being part of the third edition, were a part of this copy of the second edition as issued.

An additional complication is thus introduced into the history of the 1645 editions of Waller, for it would appear that copies of the second edition were still available from Mosley after the publication, or at least the printing, of the third edition. Perhaps, therefore, we should distinguish between two issues of the second edition, the first without, and the second with, the speeches, the change having been made in those copies of the second edition still in Mosley's hands when the more correct third edition had been printed, the sheets of the third edition being used to supply the additional matter. We might therefore give the following tentative list of the 1645 editions:

First edition		*The Workes of Edmond Waller* . . . for Thomas Walkley (including speeches)
	another issue	*Poems, &c.,* . . . T. W. for Humphrey Mosley
Second edition		*Poems, &c.,* . . . T. W. for Humphrey Mosley (without speeches)
Third edition		*Poems, &c.,* . . . I. N. for Humphrey Mosley (including speeches and claiming on the title-page to be "printed by a copy of his own hand-writing")
	another issue	on large paper (Chew)
Second edition	another issue	*Poems, &c.,* . . . T. W. for Humphrey Mosley (including speeches from sheets of 3rd ed.)

The evidence for the order of the last three entries rests upon the fortuitous survival of the contents of Don f 144 in their contemporary binding, which makes its reproduction in facsimile of particular interest. Subsequent editions appeared as follows: second edition, 1664; third edition, 1668; fourth edition, 1682; fifth edition, 1686, re-issued in 1693 and 1694; seventh edition, 1694; &c.

There is no critical edition of Waller, although according to F. W. Bateson (*Guide to English Literature,* 2nd ed. 1967) an edition by P. R. Wikelund is in preparation. Until it appears the standard edition is still that of G. Thorn-Drury, 2 vols., 1893 (Muses' Library). Nor is there a bibliography, although there is a useful paper on the 1645 editions ('The First Editions of Waller's Poems') by Beverly Chew in his *Essays and Verses about Books,* New York, 1928; though he does not distinguish between two issues of the second edition.

The Bodleian Library possesses a contemporary manuscript of Waller's poems as they first appeared in Walkley's edition of the *Workes* – MS. Don d 55 – which has been reproduced here (slightly reduced) following the facsimile of the printed book.

Reference: Wing W 512

POEMS,

&c.

WRITTEN BY

Mr. *ED. WALLER*

of *Beckonsfield*, Esquire; lately a Member of the Honourable House of Commons.

All the Lyrick Poems in this Booke were set by Mr. HENRY LAWES Gent. of the Kings Chappell, and one of his Majesties Private Musick.

Printed and Published according to Order.

LONDON,

Printed by *T.W.* for *Humphrey Mosley*, at the Princes Arms in *Pauls* Church-yard. 1645.

BIBLIOTHECA · BODLEIANA ·

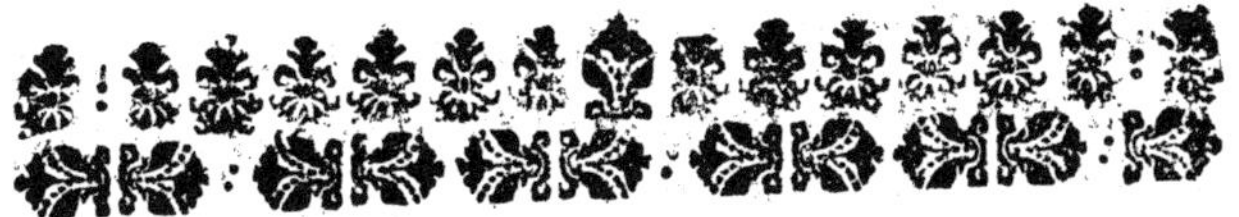

To my Lady.

MADAM,

Your Commands for the gathering of theſe ſticks into a Faggot, had ſooner been obeyed, but intending to preſent you with my whole Vintage: I ſtaied till the lateſt Grapes were ripe, for here your Ladiſhip hath not onely all I have done, but all I ever mean to doe in this kind: Not *but that I may defend the attempt I have made upon* Poetrie, *by the examples (not to trouble you with* Hiſtorie*) of many wiſe, and worthie perſons of our own times: as* Sir Philip Sidney, Sir Fra. Bacon, *Cardinall* Perron, *the ableſt of his Countrie men; and the former* Pope, *who they ſay, in ſtead of the* *triple Crown, wore ſometimes the Poets Ivy as an ornament, perhaps of leſſer weight, and trouble. But Madam, theſe Nightingales ſung only in the Spring, it was the diverſion of their youth. As Ladies learn to ſing and play when they are Children, what they forget when they are women; the reſemblance holds further: for as you quit the Lute the ſooner, becauſe the poſture is ſuſpected to draw the body awry: ſo this is not alwayes practiſed without ſome villany to the mind, wreſting it from preſent occaſions, and accuſtoming us to a Still ſomwhat removed from common uſe. But that you may not think his caſe deplorable, who had made verſes: we are told, that* Tully *(the greateſt wit among the Romans) was once ſick of this diſeaſ, & yet recovered ſo well; that of almoſt as bad a Poet as your Servant, he became the moſt perfect Orator in the world. So that not ſo much to have made verſes, as not to give over in time, leaves a man without excuſe: the former pre-*

ſenting

*ſenting us with an opportunity at leaſt of doing wiſely: that is to conceale thoſe we have made, which I ſhall yet doe, if my humble requeſt may be of as much force with your Ladiſhip, as your Commands have bin with me; Madam, I onely whiſper theſe in your ears; if you publiſh them, they are your own, and therefore as you apprehend the reproach of a Wit, and a Poet, caſt them into the fire, or if they come where green boughs are in the Chimney, with the help of your fair friends, (for thus bound, it will be too hard a task for your hands alone) to tear them in pieces, wherein you ſhall honour me with the fate of Or*pheus, *for ſo his Poems, whereof we onely beare the forme (not his limbs as the ſtory will have it) I ſuppoſe were ſcattered by the* Thracian *Dames Here Madam I might take an apportunity t celebrate your vertues, and to inſtruct you how unhappy you are, in that you know not who you are: How much you excell the moſt excellent of your own: And how*

how much you amaze the least inclined to wonder of your Sex. But as they will be apt to take your Ladiship for a Roman name: So would they believe that I indeavored the Character of a perfect Nimph, worshipt an Image of my own making, and dedicated this to the Ladie of the brain, not of the heart of your Ladiships most humble servant,

E.W.

To

An advertisement to the Reader.

READER. This parcell of exquisit Poems, have pass'd up and downe through many hands amongst persons of the best quallity, in loose imperfect Manuscripts, and there is lately obtruded to the world an adulterate Copy, surruptitiously and illegally imprinted, to the derogation of the Author, and the abuse of the Buyer. But in this Booke they appeare in their pure originals and true genuine colours. In so much that they fear not (as young Eaglets use to be tryed whither they are spurious, or of a right extraction) to look upon the

Sunne

Sunne in the Meridian, in regard *Apollo* himſelfe, the grand Patron of Poets ſeem'd not only to caſt many favourable aſpects, but by his more then ordinary influence to cooperate in their production, as will appeare to the intelligent and cleare-ſighted Reader, by that conſtant veine of *gold* (the minerall which that Planet ownes more then any other) which runnes through every one of them.

Thus they go abroad unſophiſticated, and like the preſent condition of the Author himſelfe, they are expos'd to the wide world, to travell, and try their fortunes: And I beleeve there is no gentle ſoule that pretends any thing to knowledge and the choyceſt ſort of invention but will give them entertainment and welcome.

Of His MAJESTIES *receiving the newes of the Duke of* Buckinghams *death.*

SO earnest with thy God, can no new care,
No sense of danger interrupt thy prayer?
The sacred Wrestler till a blessing given
Quits not his hold, but halting conquers heaven:
Nor was the stream of thy devotion stopp'd
When from the body such a limb was lopp'd,
As to thy present state was no lesse maime,
Though thy wise choice has since repair'd the same.
Bold *Homer* durst not so great vertue fain
In his best patterne of *Patrolus* slaine,
With such amazement as weake mothers use,
And frantick gesture he receives the news:
Yet fell his darling by th'impartiall chance
Of war, impos'd by Royall *Hectors* lance.
Thine in full peace, and by a vulgar hand
Torne from thy bosome left his high command.
The famous Painter can allow no place
For private sorrow in a Princes face:
Yet that his price might not exceed beliefe,
He cast a vail upon supposed griefe.
'Twas want of such a president as this
Made the old heathen frame their god amisse.

Their *Phœbus* should not act a fonder part
For the fair boy, then he did from his heart;
Nor blame for *Hiacinthus* fate his own (known.
That kept from him wish'd death, had'st thou bin

Yet he that weighs with thine good *Davids* deeds,
Shall finde his passion, not his love exceeds.
He curst the mountaines where his brave friend dy'd,
But left false *Ziba* with his heir divide:
Where thy mortall love to thy blest friends,
Like that of heaven upon their seed descends.
Such huge extreams inhabit thy great minde,
God-like unmov'd, and yet like woman kinde;
Which of thy ancient Poets had not brought
Our *Charles* his pedigree, from heaven and taught
How some bright dame comprest by mighty *Iove*
Produc'd this mixt divinity and love?

To the King on his Navy.

VV Here ere thy Navy spreads her canvas wings
Homage to thee, and peace to all she brings:
The French and Spaniard when thy flags appear
Forget their hatred, and consent to fear.
So *Iove* from *Ida* did both hoasts survey,
And when he pleas'd to thunder part the fray:
Ships heretofore in seas like fishes sped,
The mightiest still upon the smallest fed.
Thou on the deep impo sest stricter laws,
And by that justice hast remov'd the cause
Of those rude tempests which for rapine sent,
Too oft alas, involv'd the innocent.

Now

Now shall the Ocean as thy Thames be free
From both those fates of stormes and piracie:
But we most happy, who can fear no force
But winged troops, or Pegasean horse.
'Tis not so hard for greedy foes to spoyle
Another Nation as to touch our soyle.
Should natures selfe invade the world againe,
And ore the center spread the liquid maine:
Thy power were safe and her distructive hand,
Would but enlarge the bounds of her command.
Thy dreadfull fleet would stile thee Lord of all,
And ride in triumph ore the drowned ball.
Those towers of oake ore fertile plaines might goe
And visit mountains where they once did grow.
The worlds restorer once could not endure
That finish'd Babell should those men secure:
Whose pride design'd, that fabricks should have stood
Above the reach of any second floud.
To thee his chosen more indulgent he
Dares trust such power with so much piety.

Upon His MAJESTIES *repairing of* PAULS.

THat shipwrackt vessel which th'Apostle bore
Scarce suffer'd more upon Melitas shore,
Then did his Temple in the sea of time
(Our Nations glory, and our Nations crime.)
When the first Monarch of this happy Isle
Mov'd with the ruine of so brave a pile,
This worke of cost and piety begun
To be accomplish'd by his glorious Son;

Who all that came within the ample thought
Of his wise sire, has to perfection brought.
He like *Amphion* makes those quarries leap
Into fair figures from a confus'd heap:
For in his art of Regiments is found
A power like that of harmony in sound.

Those antique minstrels sure were *Charles* like Kings,
Cities their lutes, and subjects hearts their strings;
On which with so divine a hand they strook
Consent of motion from their breath they took.
So all our mindes with his conspire to grace
The Gentiles great Apostle, and deface
Those State observing sheds, that like a chaine
Seem'd to confine and fetter him againe;
Which the glad Saint shakes off at his command
As once the viper from his sacred hand:
So joyes the aged Oake when we divide
The creeping Ivy from his injur'd side.

Ambition rather would effect the same
Of some new structure; to have born her name
Two distant vertues in one act we finde
The modesty, and greatness of his minde;
Which not content to be above the rage
And injury of all impairing age,
In its own worth secure, doth higher clime,
And things half swallow'd from the jaws of time
Reduce an earnest of his grand designe
To frame no new Church, but the old refine:
Which Spouse-like may with comly grace command
More then by force of argument or hand.
For doubtfull reason few can apprehend,
And war brings ruine, where it should amend.

But

But beauty with a bloodlesse conquest findes
A welcome soveraignty in rudest mindes.

Not ought which *Shebas* wondring Queen beheld
Amongst the works of *Solomon* excell'd,
His ships and building; emblems of a heart
Large both in magnanimity and art:
While the propitious heavens this worke attend,
Long wanted showres they forget to send;
As if they meant to make it understood
Of more importance then our vitall food.

The Sun which riseth to salute the quire,
Already finish'd, setting shall admire
How private bounty could so far extend:
The King built all, but *Charles* the Westerne end:
So proud a fabrick to devotion given,
At once it threatneth and obligeth heaven.

Laomedon that had the gods in pay,
Neptune, with him that rules the sacred day,
Could no such structure raise, Troy wall'd so high,
Th'Atrides might as well have forc'd the sky.

Glad, though amazed, are our neighbour Kings
To see such power employ'd in peacefull things,
They list not urge it to the dreadfull field,
The taske is easier to destroy, then build.

Of the danger His Majesty *(being Prince) escaped all the rode at Saint* Andere.

NOr had his Highnesse bid farewell to *Spaine*,
And reacht the sphere of his own power the main,
With Brittish bounty in his ship he feasts,
Th'Hesperian Princes, his amazed guests;
To finde that watry wildernesse exceed
The entertainment of their great *Madrid*.
Healths to both Kings attended with the rore
Of Cannons eccho'd from th'affrighted shore;
With loud resemblance of his thunder prove
Bacchus the seed of cloud compelling *Iove*;
While to his harpe divine, *Arion* sings
The loves and conquests of our Albion Kings.
Of the fourth Edward *was his noble song,*
Fierce, goodly, valiant, beautifull and young:
He rent the Crowne from vanquisht Henries *head,*
Rais'd the White rose, and trampled on the red:
Till love triumphing ore the victors pride,
Brought Mars and Warwick to the conquer'd side:
Neglected Warwick (whose bold hand like fate
Gives and resumes the Scepter of our State)
Wooes for his master, and with double shame
Himselfe deluded, mocks the Princely dame:
The Lady Bona *whom just anger burnes,*
And forreigne war with civill rage returnes:
Ah spare your swords where beauty is too blame,
Love gave th'affront, and must repaire the same:
When France shall boast of her, whose conquering eies
Have made the best of English hearts their prize;
Have power to alter the decree of fate,
And change againe the councels of our State.

What

What the Prophetick muse intends alone
To him that feels the secret wound is knowne:
With the sweet sound of this harmonious lay
About the keele delighted Dolphins play:
Too sure a signe of Seas ensuing rage,
Which must anon this Royall troope engage:
To whom soft sleep seems more secure and sweet
Within the Towne commanded by our fleet.
These mighty Peers plac'd in the guilded Barge,
Proud with the burden of so brave a charge;
With painted oars the youth begin to sweep
Neptunes smooth face, and cleave the yeelding deep,
Which soon becomes the seat of sudden war
Between the wind and tide that fiercely jar;
As when a sort of lusty shepherds try
Their force at foot-ball, care of victory
Makes them salute so rudely breast to breast,
That their encounters seem too rough for jest.
They ply their feet, and still the restlesse ball
Tost too and fro is urged by them all.
So fares the doubtful Barge 'twixt tide and winds,
And like effect of their contention finds:
Yet the bold Britaines still securely row'd,
Charles and his vertue was their sacred load:
Then which a greater pledge heaven could not give
That the good boat, this tempest should outlive:
But storms encrease, and now no hope of grace
Among them shines, save in the Princes face.
The rest resigne their courage, skill and sight
To danger, horrour, and unwelcome night.
The gentle vessell wont with state and pride
On the smooth back of silver Thames to ride;
Wanders Astonish'd in the angry maine
As *Titans* Car did, while the golden raine

Fill'd the young hand of his adventrous son
When the whole world an equall hazard run
To this of ours: the light of whose desire,
Waves threaten now; as that was skar'd by fire,

The impatient sea grows impotent and raves
That (night assisting) his impetuous waves
Should finde resistance from so light a thing:
These surges ruine, those our safety bring.
Th'oppressed vessell doth the charge abide,
Only because assail'd on every side.
So men with rage and passion set on fire,
Trembling for haste impeach their mad desire.

The pale Iberians had expir'd with fear;
But that their wonder did divert their care,
To see the Prince with danger mov'd no more
Then with the pleasures of their court before.
God-like his courage seem'd, whom nor delight
Could soften, nor the face of death affright.
Next to the power of making tempests cease
Was in that storme, to have so calme a peace.

Great *Maro* could no greater tempest faine
When the loud windes usurping on the maine;
For any *Juno* labour'd to destroy
The hated reliques of confounded Troy:
His bold *Eneas*, on like billows tost
In a tall ship, and all his Countries lost:
Dissolves with fear, and both his hands upheld,
Proclaimes them happy whom the Greeks had quel'd.

In honourable fight our *Hero* set
In a small shallow fortune in his debt:

So neare a hope of Crowns and Scepters more
Then ever *Priam*, when he flourish'd, wore
His loynes yet full of ungot Princes, all
His glory in the bud; lets nothing fall,
That argues fear; if any thought annoyes
The gallant youth, 'tis loves untasted joyes,
And deare remembrance of that fatall glance,
For which he lately pawn'd his heart in France;
Where he had seen a brighter Nimph then she
That sprung out of his present foe; the sea
That noble ardor more then mortall fire,
The conquered ocean could not make expire;
Nor angry *Thetis*, raise her waves above
The heroique Prince, his courage, or his love.
'Twas indignation, and not feare he felt,
The shrine should perish where that Image dwelt.

Ah love forbid, the noblest of thy straine
Should not survive to let her know his paine:
Who nor his perill minding, nor his flame,
Is entertain'd with some lesse serious game
Among the bright Nimphs of the Gallique Court,
All highly borne, obsequious to her sport:
They roses seem within their early pride,
But halfe reveal, and halfe their beauties hide.
She the glad morning which her beams doth throw
Upon their smiling leafes, and gild them so.
Like bright *Aurora*, whose refulgent Ray
Foretells the fervour of ensuing day:
And warnes the shepherd with his flocks retreat
To leafie shadows from the threatned heat.

From *Cupids* string of many shafts that fled
Wing'd with those plumes which noble fame had shed;

As through the wondring world she flew and told
Of his adventures haughty, brave and bold:
Some had already touch'd the Royall maid,
But loves first summons seldome are obey'd.
Light was the wound the Princes care unknowne,
She might not, would not, yet reveale her owne.

His glorious name had so possest her ears,
That with delights, those antique tales she heares
Of *Iason, Theseus*, and such Worthies old,
As with his story best resemblance hold.

And now she viewes, as on the wall it hung
What old *Museus* so divinely sung:
Which art with life and love did so inspire
That she discernes, and favours that desire:
Which there provokes th'adventrous youth to swim,
And in *Leanders* dangers pities him;
Whose not new love alone but fortune seeks
To frame his story like that amorous Greeks.

For from the sterne of some good ship appears,
A friendly light which moderates their fears:
New courage from reviving hope they take,
And climbing ore the waves that taper make;
On which the hope of all their lives depends,
As his on that fair *Heroes* hand extends.

The Ship at anchor like a fixed rock
Breaks the proud billows which her large sides knock;
Whose rage restrained foming higher swells,
And from her port the weary barge repells;
Threatning to make her forced out againe,
Repeat the dangers of the troubled maine.

Twice

Twice was the cable hurl'd in vaine; the fates
Would not be moved for our sister States:
For *England* is the third successefull throw,
And then the Genius of that Land they know:
Whose Prince must be (as their owne books devise)
Lord of the Scene, where now the danger lies.
Well sung the Roman Bard, all human things
Of dearest value hang on slender strings.
O see the then sole hope, and in designe
Of heaven our joy supported by a line:
Which for that instant was heavens care above
The chaine thats fixed to the throne of *Jove*;
On which the fabricke of our world depends,
One linck dissolv'd, the whole creation ends.

To the QUEEN, *occasioned upon sight of her* MAJESTIES *Picture.*

WEll fare the hand which to our humble sight
Presents that beauty which the dazling light
Of Royall splendor hides from weaker eyes:
And all excesse (save by this art) denies.
Here only we have courage to behold
This beam of glory, here we dare unfold
In numbers thus the wonders we conceive;
The gracious Image seeming to give leave
Propitious stands, vouchsafing to be seen;
And by our muse saluted
Mighty Queen.

In whom th'extreams of power and beauty move
The Queen of Brittain and the Queen of Love.

As the bright Sun (to which we owe no sight)
Of equal glory to your beauties light,
Is wisely plac'd in so sublime a seat
T'extend his light, and moderate his heat.
So happy 'tis you move in such a sphere
As your h gh Majesty with awfull fear,
In humane breasts might qualifie that fire
Which kindled by those eyes had flamed higher,
Then when the scorched world like hazard run
By the approach of the ill guided Sun.
No other Nimphs have title to mens hearts,
But as their meannesse larger hope imparts :
Your beauty more the fondest lover moves
With admiration then his private loves ;
With admiration for a pitch so high
(Save sacred *Charles* his) never love durst flye.
Heaven that preferr'd a Scepter to your hand
Favour'd our freedome, more then your command.
Beauty had crown'd you, and you must have bin
The whole worlds mistris, other then a Queen.
All had bin Rivals ; and you might have spar'd,
Or kill'd and tyranniz'd without a guard.
No power atchiev'd, either by arms or birth
Equalls loves empire, both in heaven and earth.
Such eyes as yours, on *Jove* himselfe have throwne
As bright and fierce a lightning as his owne :
Witnesse our *Jove* prevented by their flame
In his swift passage to the Hesperian dame,
When (like a Lion) finding in his way
To some intended spoile a fairer prey.
The Royall youth pursuing the report
Of beauty, found it in the Gallique Court :
There publique care with private passion fought
A doubtfull combate in his noble thought,

Should

Should he confesse his greatnesse, and his love,
And the free faith of your great brother prove,
With his Achates breaking through the cloud
Of that disguise which did their graces shroud;
And mixing with those gallants at the ball,
Dance with the Ladies and outshine them all:
Or on his journey ore the mountaines ride;
So when the fair *Leucothee* he espy'd
To check his steeds; impatient *Phebus* earn'd,
Though all the world was in his wars concern'd.
What may hereafter her meridian doe,
Whose dawning beauty warm'd his bosome so:
Not so divine a flame, since deathlesse gods
Forbore to visit the defil'd abodes
Of men, in any mortall breast did burne,
Nor shall till piety and they returne.

The Apology of sleep:

For not approaching the Lady who can do any thing but sleep when she pleaseth.

MY charge it is, those breaches to repaire
Which nature takes from sorrow, toil and care.
Rest to the limbs and quiet, I confer
On troubled mindes; but nought can adde to her
Whom heaven & her transcendent thoughts have plac'd
Above those ills which wretched mortals taste.

Bright as the deathlesse gods, and happy she
From all that may infringe delight, is free:

Love

Love at her Royall feet his quiver layes,
And not his mother with more haste obeyes.
Such reall pleasures, such true joyes suspence,
What dream can I present to recompence?

Should I with lightning fill her awfull hands,
And make the clouds seem all at her commands;
Or place her in *Olimpus* top, a guest
Among th'mortalls who with Nectar feast:
That power would seem that entertainment short
Of the true splendor of her present Court;
Where all the joyes and all the glories are
Of three great Kingdomes, sever'd from the care.
I that of fumes and humid vapours made,
Ascending doe the seat of sense invade.
No cloud in so serene a mansion finde,
To over-cast her ever shining minde,
Which holds resemblance with those spotlesse skies,
Where flowing *Nilus* want of raine supplies.
That christal heaven, where *Phœbus* never shrouds
His golden beams, nor wraps his face in clouds.

But what so hard which numbers cannot force,
So stoops the moon, and rivers change their course.
The bold *Mæonian* made me dare to steep
Joves dreadfull temples in the dew of sleep.
And since the Muses do invoke my power,
I shall no more decline that sacred bower
Where *Gloriana* their great mistresse lyes,
But gently taming those victorious eyes,
Charme all her senses; till the joyfull Sun
Without a rivall halfe his course has run:
Who while my hand that fairer light confines
May boast himself the brightest thing that shines.

The

The Country to my Lady of Carlile.

Madam:

OF all the sacred Muse inspir'd,
Orpheus alone could with the woods comply;
Their rude inhabitants his song admir'd,
And natures selfe in those that could lye.
Your beauty next our solitude invades,
And warms us shining, through thickest shades.

Nor ought the tribute which the wondring Court,
Paies your fair eies, prevail with you to scorne
The answer and consent to the report
Which eccho-like the Country doth return.
Mirrors are taught to flatter, but our springs
Present th'impartiall images of things.

A rurall judge dispos'd of beauties prize,
A simple shepherd was preferr'd to *Jove*,
Down to the mountains from the partial skies
Came *Juno*, *Pallas* and the Queen of Love,
To plead for that which was so justly given
To the bright *Carlile* of the Court of Heaven.

Carlile a name which all our words are taught,
Loud as his Amarillis to resound.
Carlile a name which on the barke is wrought
Of every tree thats worthy of the wound.
From *Phœbus* rage, our shadows, and our streams,
May guard us better then from *Carliles* beams.

The Countesse of Carlile *in mourning.*

WHen from black clouds no part of skie is clear
But just so much as lets the Sun appear:
Heavens then would seem thy image, and reflect
Those sable vestments, and that bright aspect.
A sparke of vertue by the deepest shade
Of sad adversity is fairer made;
Nor lesse advantage doth thy beauty get
A *Venus* rising from a sea of jet.
Such was the appearance of new formed light
While yet it strugled with eternall night:
Then mourne no more lest thou admit encrease
Of glory by thy noble Lords decease.
We finde not that the laughter loving dame
Mourn'd for *Anchises*; 'twas enough she came
To grace the mortall with her deathlesse bed,
And that his living eyes such beauty fed:
Had she bin there, untimely joy through all
Mens hearts diffus'd, had mar'd the funerall.
Those eyes were made to banish griefe: as well
Bright *Phœbus* might affect in shades to dwell,
As they to put on sorrow; nothing stands
But power to grieve, exempt from thy commands:
If thou lament, thou must doe so alone
Griefe in thy presence, can lay hold on none:
Yet still persist the memory to love
Of that great Mercury of our mighty *Jove*:
Who by the power of his enchanting tongue
Swords from the hands of threatning Monarchs wrung
War he presented, or soon made it cease,
Instructing Princes in the arts of peace:

Such

Such as made *Sheba's* curious Queen resort
To the large hearted Hebrews famous Court.
Had *Homer* sate among his wondring guests,
He might have learn'd at those stupendious feasts,
With greater bounty, and more sacred state
The banquet of the gods to celebrate.
But O ! what elocution might he use,
What potent charms that could so soon infuse
His absent masters love into the heart
Of *Henrietta* forcing her to part
From her lov'd Brother, Country, and the Sun,
And like *Camilla* ore the waves to run
Into his armes, while the Parisian dames
Mourn for their ravish't glory at her flames ?
No lesse amaz'd, then the amazed stars,
When the bold charmer of Thessalia wars
With heaven it self, and numbers does repeat,
Which call discending *Cinthia* from her seat.

In answer to, &c.

WHat fury has provok't thy wit to dare
With *Diomed*, to wound the Queen of Love
Thy mistris Envy, or thine own despair ?
Not the just *Pallas* in th breast did move.
So blinde a rage with such a different fate,
He honour won, where thou hast purchast hate.

She gave assistance to his Trojan foe ;
Thou that without a rivall thou maiest love,
Dost to the beauty of thy Lady owe,

While after her the gazing world does move.
Canst thoū not be content to love alone,
Or is thy mistris not content with one?

Hast thou not read of fairy *Arthurs* shield,
Which but disclos'd, amaz'd the weaker eyes
Of proudest foe, and won the doubtfull field?
So shall thy Rebell wit become her prize.
Should thy Iambecks swell into a book,
All were confuted with one Radiant look.

Heaven he oblig'd that place her in the skies,
Rewarding *Phœbus*, for inspiring so
His noble braine by likening to those eyes
His joyfull beams, but *Phœbus* is thy foe:
And neither ayds thy fancy nor thy sight,
So ill thou rim'st against so faire a light.

On my Lady Dorothy Sidneyes *Picture:*

SUch was *Philoclea*, and such *Dorus* flame,
The matchlesse *Sidney* that immortall frame
Of perfect beauty on two pillars plac't;
Not his high fancy could one patterne grac't:
With such extreams of excellence compose
Wonders so distant in one face disclose:
Such cheerfull modesty, such humble state,
Moves certaine love, but with as doubtfull fate;
As when beyond our greedy reach we see
Inviting fruit on too sublime a tree.
All the rich flowers through his *Arcadia* found
Amaz'd we see, in this one garland bound.

Had but this copy which the Artists tooke
From the fair picture of that noble Book,
Stood at *Calanders* the brave friends had jarr'd,
And Rivalls made, the ensuing story marr'd.
Just nature first instructed by his thought
In his own house thus practiz'd what he taught.
This glorious piece transcends what he could think ;
So much his blood is nobler then his ink.

To Vandike.

RAre *Artisan*, whose pensill moves
Not our delights alone, but loves :
From thy shop of beauty, we
Slaves return that enter'd free.
The headlesse lover does not know
Whose eyes they are that wound him so :
But confounded with thy art,
Inquires her name that has his heart :
Another who did long refrain
Feels his old wound bleed fresh again ;
With deare remembrance of that face,
Where now he reads new hopes of grace :
Nor scorne, nor cruelty does finde,
But gladly suffers a false winde
To blow the ashes of despaire
From the reviving brand of care :
Foole that forget'st her stubborne looke,
This softnesse from thy finger tooke :
Strange that thy hand should not inspire
The beauty onely but the fire :

Not the form alone and grace,
But act and power of a face:
May'st thou yet thy selfe as well,
As all the world beside excell;
So thou th'unfeigned truth rehearse
(That I may make it live in verse)
Why thou couldst not at one assay
That face to after times convey,
Which this admires; was it thy wit
To make her oft before thee sit?
Confesse, and we'll forgive thee this,
For who would not repeat that blisse,
And frequent sight of such a dame
Buy with the hazard of his fame?
Yet who can tax thy blamelesse skill,
Though thy good hand had failed still?
When natures self so often errs,
She for this many thousand years
Seems to have practis'd with much care,
To frame the race of women fair;
Yet never could a perfect birth
Produce before to grace the earth:
Which waxed old ere it could see
Her that amaz'd thy art and thee.
  But now 'tis done, O let me know
Where those immortall colours grow,
That could this deathless piece compose
In Lillies, or the fading Rose:
No for this theft thou hast clim'd higher
Then did *Prometheus* for his fire.

At

At Pens-hurst.

WHile in this Park I sing, the listning Deer
Attend my passion, and forget to fear.
When to the Beeches I report my flame,
They bow their heads as if they felt the same:
To Gods appealing, when I reach their bowres
With loud complaints, they answer me in showres.
To thee a wilde and cruell soule is given,
More deaf then trees, and prouder then the heaven.
Loves so profest, why dost thou falsely fain
Thy self a *Sidney*? from which noble strain
He sprung, that could so far exalt the name
Of love, and warm our Nation with his flame:
That all we can of love or high desire,
Seems but the smoak of amorous *Sidneyes* fire.
Nor call her mother, who so well do prove,
One breast may hold both chastity and love.
Never can she, that so exceeds the spring
In joy and bounty, be suppos'd to bring
One so destructive, to no humane stock
We owe this fierce unkindness; but the rock,
That cloven rock produc'd thee, by whose side
Nature to recompence the fatall pride
Of such stern beauty, plac'd those healing springs
Which not more help then that destruction brings.
Thy heart no ruder then the rugged stone,
I might like *Orpheus* with my numerous moan
Melt to compassion; now my traitrous song,
With thee conspires to do the singer wrong:
While thus I suffer not my self to lose
The memory of what augments my woes:

But with my owne breath ſtill foment the fire
Which flames as high as fancy can aſpire.
This laſt complaint th'indulgent ears did pierce
Of juſt *Apollo*, Preſident of Verſe,
Highly concerned, that the Muſe ſhould bring
Damage to one whom he had taught to ſing:
Thus he adviſ'd me on yon aged tree,
Hang up thy Lute, and high thee to the Sea,
That there with wonders thy diverted minde
Some truce at leaſt may with affection finde.
Ah cruell Nimph from whom her humble ſwaine
Flies for reliefe unto the raging maine:
And from the windes and tempeſts doth expect
A milder fate then from her cold neglect:
Yet there he'll pray that the unkinde may prove
Bleſt in her choice, and vows this endleſſe love
Springs from no hope of what ſhe can confer
But from thoſe gifts which heaven has heap'd on her.

At Penſ-hurſt.

HAd *Dorothea* liv'd when mortals made
Choice of their deities, this ſacred ſhade
Had held an altar to her power that gave
The peace and glory, which theſe allays have
Embroydred ſo with flowers where ſhe ſtood,
That it became a garden of the wood:
Her preſence has ſuch more then humane grace
That it can civilize the rudeſt place,
And beauty too, and order can impart
Where nature nere intended it, nor art.

The

The plants acknowledge this, and her admire
No less then those of old did *Orpheus* Lire:
If she sit downe with tops all toward her bow'd,
They round about her into arbours crowd:
Or if she walk, in even ranks they stand
Like some well marshall'd and obsequious band.
Amphion so made stones and timber leap
Into fair figures from a confus'd heap:
And in the symetry of her parts is found
A power like that of harmony in sound:
Yee lofty beeches tell this matchlesse dame
That if together ye feed all on one flame;
It could not equalize the hundred part
Of what her eyes have kindled in my heart.
Goe boy and carve this passion on the bark
Of yonder tree, which stands the sacred mark
Of noble *Sidneyes* birth; when such benigne,
Such more then mortall making stars did shine;
That there they cannot but for ever prove
The monument and pledge of humble love:
His humble love whose hope shall nere rise higher
Then for a pardon that he dares admire.

To my Lord of Leicester.

NOt that thy trees at Pens-hurst grove
Oppressed with their timely load,
And seem to make their silent moan,
That their great Lord is now abroad:
They to delight his taste or eye
Would spend themselves in fruit and dye.

Not that thy harmless Deer repine,
And think themselves unjustly slain
By any other hand then thine,
Whose arrows they would gladly slain:
No nor thy friends which hold too dear
That peace with France which keeps thee there.

All these are lesse then that great cause,
Which none exacts your presence here,
Wherein there meet the divers laws
Of publick and domestick care.
For one bright Nimph our youth contends,
And on your prudent choice depends.

Not the bright shield of *Thetis* Sun,
For which such stern debate did rise,
That the Great *Ajax*, *Telemon*
Refus'd to live without the prize.
Those Achave Peers did more engage,
Then she the gallants of our age.

That beam of beauty which begun
To warm us so when thou wert here,
Now scorches like the raging Sun
When *Syrius* does first appear.
O fix this flame, and let despair
Redeem the rest from endlesse care!

To my young Lady Lucy Sidney.

VV Hy came I so untimely forth
Into a world which wanting thee

Could

Could entertain us with no worth
Or ſhadow of felicity?
  That time ſhould me ſo far remove
  From that which I was born to love.

Yet faireſt bloſſome do not ſlight
That age which you muſt know ſo ſoon,
The roſie morne reſignes her light,
And milder glory to the Moon:
  And then what wonders ſhall you do,
  Whoſe dawning beauty warms us ſo?

Hope waits upon the flowry prime,
And ſummer though it be leſs gay,
Yet is not look't on as a time
Of declination or decay.
  For with a full hand that doth bring
  All that was promis'd by the ſpring.

Of the Lady who can ſleep when ſhe pleaſes.

NO wonder ſleep from carefull lovers flies
To bathe himſelf in *Sachariſſa's* eyes,
As fair *Aſtrea* once from earth to heaven
By ſtrife and loud impiety was driven:
So with our plaints offended, and our tears
Wiſe *Somnus* to that Paradiſe repairs,
Waits on her will, and wretches does forſake
To court the Nimph for whom thoſe wretches wake:
More proud then *Phœbus* of his throne of gold
Is the ſoft god thoſe ſofter limbs to hold.

Nor

Nor would exchange with *Jove* to hide the skies
In darkning clouds the power to close her eyes ;
Eyes which so far all other lights controul,
They warm our mortall parts, but these our soul :
Let her free spirit whose unconquer'd breast
Holds such deep quiet and untroubled rest :
Know that though *Venus* and her son should spare
Her Rebell heart, and never teach her care :
Yet Hymen may inforce her vigils keep,
And for anothers joy suspend her sleep.

Of the mis-report of her being painted.

AS when a sort of Wolves infest the night
With their wilde howlings at fair *Cinthia*'s light,
The noyse may chase sweet slumber from our eyes,
But never reach the mistresse of the skies :
So with the news of *Sacharissa*'s wrongs,
Her vexed servants blame those envious tongues:
Call love to witnesse that no painted fire
Can scorch men so, or kindle such desire :
While unconcerned she seems mov'd no more
With this new malice then our loves before :
But from the height of her great minde looks down
On both our passions without smile or frown :
So little care of what is done below
Hath the bright dame whom heaven affecteth so,
Paints her : 'tis true with the same hand which spreads
Like glorious colours through the flowry meads.
When lavish nature with her best attire
Clothes the gay spring, the season of desire.

Paints

Paints her, 'tis true, and does her cheek adorne
With the same art wherewith she paints the morne:
With the same art wherewith she gildeth so
Those painted clouds which forme *Thaumantias* bow.

Of her passing through a crowd of people.

As in old Chaos Heaven with earth confus'd,
And stars with rocks together crush'd and bruis'd,
The Sun his light no further could extend
Then the next hill which on his shoulders lean'd:
So in this throng bright *Sacharissa* far'd,
Oppress'd by those who strove to be her guard;
As ships though never so obsequious, fall
Foul in a tempest on their Admirall:
A greater favour this disorder brought
Unto her servants then their awfull thought
Durst entertain, when thus compell'd they prest
The yeelding marble of her snowy breast:
While love insults disguised in a cloud,
And welcome force of the unruly croud.
So th'amorous tree while yet the air is calm
Just distance keeps from his desired palm.
But when the wind her ravish't branches throws
Into her arms, and mingles all their bows:
Though loath he seems her tender leaves to presse,
More loath he is that friendly storm should cease:
From whose rude bounty, he the double use
At once receives of pleasure and excuse.

SONG.

SONG.

Say lovely dream, where couldst thou finde
Shades to counterfeit that face?
Colours of this glorious kinde,
Come not from any mortall race.

In heaven it self thou sure wer't drest
With that Angel-like disguise;
Thus deluded am I blest,
And see my joy with closed eyes.

But ah this Image is too kinde
To be other then a dream!
Cruell *Sacharissa's* minde
Never put on that sweet extream.

Fair dream if thou intend'st me grace
Change that heavenly face of thine;
Paint despis'd love in thy face,
And make it to appear like mine.

Pale, wan, and meager let it look,
With a pity moving shape,
Such as wander by the brook
Of Lethe, or from graves escape.

Then to that matchless Nimph appear,
In whose shape thou shinest so
Softly in her sleeping ear,
With humble words express my wo.

Perhaps

Perhaps from greatness, state, and pride,
Thus surprised she may fall:
Sleep does disproportion hide,
And death resembling equalls all.

SONG.

BEhold the brand of beauty tost;
See how the motion does delate the flame.
Delighted love his spoyls does boast,
And triumph in this game.
Fire to no place confin'd,
Is both our wonder and our fear,
Moving the mind,
Like lightning hurled through the air.

High heaven the glory does encrease
Of all her shining lamp this artfull way,
The Sun in figures such as these
Joyes with the Moon to play.
To the sweet strains they advance,
Which do result from their own fears
As the Nimphs dance,
Moves with the numbers which she hears.

To Amorett.

FAir that you may truly know
What you unto *Thirsis* ow,

I will

I will tell you how I do
Sacharissa love and you.

Joy salutes me when I set
My blest eyes on *Amorett:*
But with wonder I am strook
When I on the other look.

If sweet *Amoret* complains,
I have sence of all her pains;
But for *Sacharissa*, I
Do not onely grieve, but die.

All that of my selfe is mine
Lovely *Amoret* is thine;
Sacharissa's captive faine
Would untie his iron chaine.

And those scorching beames to shun
To thy gentle shadow run:
If the soule had free election
To dispose of her affection,
I would not thus long have born
Haughty *Sacharissa*'s scorne;
But 'tis some pure power above,
Which controuls our will in love.

If not love, a strong desire
To create and spread that fire
In my breasts, solicites me
Beauteous *Amoret* for thee.

'Tis amazement more then love
Which her radiant eyes doe move;

If

If lesse splendor wait on thine,
Yet they so benignly shine.

I would turne my dazelled sight
To behold their milder light,
But as hard 'tis to destroy
That high flame, as to enjoy;
Which, how easily I may doe
Heaven (as easily seal'd) do'es know:
Amoret as sweet and good
As the most delicious food,
Which but tasted doth impart
Life and goodnesse to the heart.
Sacharissa's beauty, wine,
Which to madnes doth incline:
Such a liquor as no brain
That is mortall can sustain.
Scarce can I to Heaven excuse
That Devotion which I use
Unto that adored Dame;
For 'tis not unlike the same
Which I thither ought to send;
So that if it could take end
'Twould to Heaven it self be due
To succeed her and not you,
Who already have of me
All that's not Idolatry;
Which though not so fierce a flame
Is longer like to be the same.

Then smile on me, and I will prove,
Wonder is shorter liv'd, then Love.

The story of Phœbus *and* Daphne *appli'd.*

THirsis a youth of the inspired train,
Fair *Sacharissa* lov'd, but lov'd in vain:
Like *Phœbus* sung the no lesse amorous boy,
Like *Daphne* she as lovely and as coy:
With numbers he the flying Nimph pursues,
With numbers such as *Phœbus* self might use:
Such is the chase when love and fancy leads
Ore craggy mountains, and through flowry meads;
Invoke to testifie the lovers care,
Or form some image of his cruell fair:
Urg'd with his fury like a wounded Deer,
Ore these he fled, and none approaching near:
Had reacht the Nimph with his harmonious lay,
Whom all his charms could not incline to stay.
Yet what he sung in his immortall strain,
Though unsuccessfull, was not sung in vain:
All but the Nimph that should redress his wrong,
Attend his passion, and approve his song.
  Like *Phœbus* thus acquiring unsought praise,
  He catcht at love, and fill'd his arm with bayes.

Of Mrs. Ardea,

BEhold, and listen while the fair
Breaks in sweet sounds and willing air,
And with her own breath fans the fire
Which her bright eyes do first inspire;

What

What reason can that love controul,
Which more then one way courts the soul?

So when a flash of lightening falls
On our abodes, the danger calls
For humane aid, which hopes the flame
To conquer, though from heaven it came.
But if the wind with that conspire,
Men strive not, but deplore the fire.

On the discovery of a Ladies painting.

PIgmaleons fate reverst is mine,
His marble love took flesh and blood;
All that I worship is divine:
That beauty now 'tis understood,
Appears to have no more of life
Then that whereof he fram'd his wife.

As women yet who apprehend
Some sudden cause of causless fear,
Although that seeming cause take end,
And they behold no danger near:
A shaking through their limbs they finde
Like leaves saluted by the winde.

So though the beauty do appear,
No beauty which amaz'd me so,
Yet from my breast I cannot tear
The passion which from thence did grow,
Nor yet out of my fancy rase
The print of that supposed face.

A reall beauty though too neer,
The fond *Narcissus* did admire;
I dote on that which is no where,
The sign of beauty feeds my fire;
No mortal flame was ere so cruell
As this which thus survives the fuell.

To a Lady from whom he received a Silver Pen.

Madam,

INtending to have tride
The silver favor which you gave,
In ink the shining point I di'd,
And drencht it in the sable wave:
When griev'd to be so foully stain'd,
On you it thus to me complain'd.

Suppose you had deserv'd to take
From her fair hand so fair a boon,
Yet how deserved I to make
So ill a change, who ever woon
Immortall praise for what I wrought,
Instructed by her noble thought.

I that expressed her commands
To mighty Lords and Princely Dames,
Alwayes most welcome to their hands,
Proud that I would record their names,
Must now be taught an humble stile
Some meaner beauty to beguile.

So

So I the wronged pen to please,
 Make it my humble thanks expresse
Unto your Ladiship in these,
 And now 'tis forced to confess
That your great self did nere indite;
Nor that to one more noble write.

On a brede of divers colours, woven by foure Ladyes.

TWice twenty slender virgin finger twine,
 This curious web where all their fancies shine;
As Nature them, so they this shade have wrought
Soft as their hands, and various as their thought.
Not *Juno*'s bird when his fair train dispread,
He woes the Female to his painted bed:
No not the bow which so adorns the skies,
So glorious is, or boasts so many dies.

On the head of a Stag.

SO we some antick *Hero*'s strength
Learn by his Launces, weight and length;
As these vast beams expresse the beast,
Whose shady brows alive they drest.
Such game while yet the world was new,
The mighty *Nimrod* did pursue.
What Huntsman of our feeble race,
Or dogs dare such a monster chase?

Resembling with each blow he strikes
The change of a whole troop of Pikes:
O fertile head which every year
Could such a crop of wonder bear!
The teeming earth did never bring
So soon, so hard, so huge a thing;
Which might it never have been cast
Each years growth added to the last:
These lofty branches had supply'd
The earths bold sons prodigious pride:
Heaven with these engines had been scal'd
When mountains heap'd on mountains fail'd.

To a Lady in retirement.

SEes not my love how time resumes
The glory which he lent these flowers;
Though none should taste their sweet perfumes,
Yet must they live but some few hours,
Time what we forbear devours.

Had *Hellen*, or th'Egyptian Queen,
Been nere so thrifty of their graces,
Those beauties must at length have been
The spoyl of age which findes out faces
In the most retired places.

Should some malignant Planet bring
A barren drought or ceaseless shower
Upon the Autumn or the Spring;
And spare us neither fruit nor flower,
Winter would not stay an hour.

Could

Could the resolve of loves neglect
Preserve ye from the violation
Of comming years then more respect
  Were due to so divine a fashion,
  Nor would I divulge my passion.

The Misers speech in a Mask.

BAlls of this mettal slack'd *Atlanta's* pace,
And on the amorous youth bestow'd the race:
Venus, the Nimphs minde measuring by her own,
Whom the rich spoyls of Cities overthrown
Had prostrated to *Mars* could well advise
Th'adventrous lover how to gain the prise:
Nor less may *Jupiter* to gold ascribe,
When he turn'd himself into a bribe:
Who can blame *Diana*, or the brazen tower,
That they which stood not the Almighty showre;
Never till then did love make *Jove* put on
A form more bright and noble then his own?
Nor were it just would he resume that shape
That slack devotion should his thunder scape.
'Twas not revenge for griev'd *Apolloes* wrong
Those Asses ears on *Mida's* Temple hung;
But fond repentance of his happy wish,
Because his meat grew mettal like his dish.
Would *Bacchus* bless me so, Ide constant hold
Unto my wish, and dye creating gold.

To my Lord of Northumberland upon the death of his Lady.

TO this great losse a Sea of Tears is due,
But the whole debt not to be paid by you:
Charge not your self with all, nor render vain
Those showers the eyes of us your servants rain.
Shall grief contract the largeness of that heart,
In which, nor fear nor anger has a part?
Vertue would blush, if time should boast (which cries,
Her sole child dead their tender mothers eyes)
Your mindes relief, where reason triumphs so
Over all passions, that they nere could grow
Beyond their limits in your noble breast,
To harm another, or impeach your rest.
This we observ'd, delighting to obey
One who did never from his great self stray:
Whose milde example seemed to engage
Th'obsequious Seas, and teach them not to rage.
The brave *Emilius* his great charge laid down,
(The force of *Rome*, and fate of *Macedon*)
In his lost sons did feel, the cruell stroke
Of changing fortune, and thus highly spoke
Before *Romes* people; we did oft implore
That if the Heavens had any ill in store,
For your *Emilius* they would pour it still
On his own House, and let you flourish still:
You on the barren Sea (my Lord) have spent,
Whole Springs and Summers to the publick lent:

Suspended

Suspended all the pleasures of your life,
And shortned the short joy of such a wife:
For which your Countrey's more obliged then
For many lives of old, less happy men.
You that have sacrific'd so great a part
Of youth and private bliss, ought to impart
Your sorrow too and give your friends a right
As well in your affliction, as delight:
Then with *Emilian* courage bear this cross,
Since publick persons onely publick loss
Ought to affect, and though her form and youth,
Her application to your will and truth,
That noble sweetness, and that humble state
All snatcht away by such a hasty fate,
Might give excuse to any common brest,
With the huge weight of so such grief opprest.
Yet let no portion of your life be stain'd
With passion, but your character maintain'd
To the last act; it is enough her Stone
May honored be with superscription
Of the sole Lady, who had power to move
The Great *Nothumberland* to grieve and love.

To my Lord Admiral of his late sicknesse and Recovery.

WIth joy like ours the Thracian youth invades
Orpheus returning from th' *Elizian* shades,
Embrace the *Hero*, and his stay implore,
Make it their publick suit, he would no more

Desert them so, and for his Spouses sake,
His vanish't love tempt the Lethean lake:
The Ladies too the brightest of that time,
 Ambitious all his lofty bed to clime.
Their doubtfull hopes with expectation feed
Who shall the fair *Euridice* succeed:
Euridice for whom his num'rous moan
Makes listning trees, and salvage mountains groan:
Through all the air his sounding strings dilate
Sorrow like that which touch our hearts of late:
Your pining sickness, and your restless pain,
At once the Land affecting, and the main,
When the glad news that you were Admiral.
Scarce through the Nation spread 'twas fear'd by all:
That our Great *Charles*, whose wisdom shines in you,
Would be perplexed how to chuse anew.
So more then private was the joy and grief,
That at the worst, it gave our souls relief:
That in our age such sense of vertue liv'd,
They joy'd so justly, and so justly griev'd:
Nature her fairest lights eclipsed seems
Her self to suffer in those sharp extreams;
While not from thine alone thy blood retires,
But from those cheeks which all the world admires,
The stem thus threatned, and the sap in thee
Droop all the branches of that noble Tree:
Their beauty they and we our loves suspend,
Nought can our wishes, save thy health intend:
A Lillies overcharg'd with rain they bend
Their beauteous heads, and with high heaven contend,
Fold thee within their snowy arms, and cry
He is too faultless, and too young to dye;
So like immortals round about thee they
Sit, that they fright approaching death away:

Who

Who would not languish by so fair a train,
To be lamented and restor'd again?
  Or thus with-held, what hasty soul would go,
Though to the blest, ore young *Adonis* so?
Fair *Venus* mourn'd, and with the pretious showre
Of her warm tears cherish't the springing flower.
  The next support fair hope of your great name,
And second pillar of that noble frame:
By loss of thee wou'd no advantage have,
But step by step pursues thee to the grave.
  And now relentless fate about to end
The line which backward does so far extend,
That antick stock which still the world supplies
With bravest spirits, and with brightest eyes.
Kinde *Phœbus* interposing bid me say
Such storms no more shall shake that house, but they
Like *Neptune*, and his Sea-born Neece shall be
The shining glories of the Land and Sea:
With courage guard, and beauty warm our age,
And lovers fill with like Poetick rage.

On the friendship betwixt Sacharissa *and* Amorett.

TEll me lovely loving paire,
Why so kinde, and so severe?
Why so careless of our care,
Onely to prove selves so dear?

By this cunning change of hearts,
You the power of love controul,
While the boyes deluded darts,
Can arrive at neither soul.

For in vain to either breast
Still beguiled love does come,
Where he findes a forrain ghuest,
Neither of your hearts at home.

Debtors thus with like designe,
When they never mean to pay:
That they may the Law decline,
To some friend make all away.

Not the silver Doves that flie,
Yoak't in *Cytharea's* Car,
Not the wings that lift so high,
And convey her son so far.

Are so lovely, sweet, and fair,
Or do more enable love,
Are so choicely matcht a pair,
Or with more content to move.

A la Malade.

AH lovely *Amoret* the care
Of all that know whats good or fair:
Is Heaven become our Rival too,
Had the rich gifts conferr'd on you,

So

So amply thence the common end,
Of giving Lovers to pretend.
  Hence to this pining sicknes (meant
  To weary thee to a consent
Of leaving us) no power is given,
Thy beauties to impair the heaven:
Solicites thee with such a care,
As Roses from their stalks we tare:
When we would still preserve them new,
And fresh as on the bush they grew.
  With such a grace you entertain,
And look with such contempt on pain
That languish in you, conquer more,
And wound us deeper then before.
The lightnings which in storms appear,
Scorch more then when the skies are clear.
And as pale sicknes does invade
Your frailer part, the breaches made
In that fair lodging still more clear,
Make the bright ghuest your soul appear:
So Nimphs ore pathless mountains born,
Their light robes by the brambles torn
From their fair limbs, exposing new
And unknown beauties to the view,
Of following gods increase their flame,
And haste to catch the flying Game.

Of her Chamber.

THey taste of death that do at Heaven arive,
But we this Paradise approach alive.

Instead

Instead of death, the dart of love does strike;
And renders all within, these walls alike:
The high in titles, and the shepheard here
Forgets his greatness, and forgets his fear:
All stand amaz'd and gazing on the fair,
Loose thought of what themselves or others are:
Ambition loose, and have no other scope,
Save *Carliles* favour to imploy their hope.
The Thracian could (though all those tales were true
The bold Greeks tell) no greater wonders do,
Before his feet, so sheep and Lions lay
Fearless and wrathless, while they heard him play
The Gay, the Wise, the Gallant, and the Grave,
Subdu'd alike all, but one passion have:
No worthy minde but findes in hers there is
Something proportion'd to the rule of his:
Whilest she with cheerful, but impartial grace,
(Born for no one, but to delight the race
Of men) liks *Phœbus*, so divides her light,
And warms us that she stoops not from her height.

Of loving at first sight.

NOt caring to observe the winde,
Or the new Sea explore,
Snatch't from my self how far behinde,
Already I behold the shore.

May not a thousand dangers sleep
In the smooth bosome of this deep?
No: 'tis so rockless, and so clear,
That the rich bottome does appear

Pav'd

Pav'd all with pretious things not torn
From shipwrackt vessels, but there born.

Sweetness, truth, and every grace,
Which time and youth are wont to teach,
The eye may in a moment reach,
And read distinctly in her face
Some other Nimph with colours faint,
And pensil slow may *Cupid* paint;
And a weak heart in time destroy,
She has a stamp and prints the boy,
Can with a single look inflame
The coldest breast, the rudest tame:

The selfe banished:

IT is not that I love you lesse
Then when before your feet I lay:
But to prevent the sad encrease
Of hopeless love, I keep away.

In vain (alas) for every thing
Which I have known belong to you:
Your form does to my fancy bring,
And make my old wounds bleed anew.

Whom the Spring from the new Sun,
Already has a Feavor got:
Too late begins those shafts to shun
Which *Phœbus* through his veins has shot:

Too late he would the pain asswage,
And to thick shadows does retire;
About with him he bears the rage,
And in his tainted blood the fire.

But vow'd I have, and never must
Your banish'd servant trouble you;
For if I break you may mistrust
The vow I make to love you too.

Of the Queen.

THe Lark that shuns on lofty bough to build
Her humble Nest, lies silent in the Field:
But if the promise of a cloudless day,
Aurora smiling bids her rise and play:
Then straight she shews 'twas not for want of voice,
Or power to climb, she made so low a choice:
Singing she mounts, her angry wings are stretch't
Towards heaven, as if from heaven her note she fetcht.

So we retiring from the busie throng,
Use to restrain th'ambition of our song;
But since the light which now informs our age
Breaks from the court indulgent to her rage:
Thither my Muse, like bold *Prometheus* flyes
To light her torch at *Gloriana*'s eyes.

Those sovereign beams which heal the wounded soul,
And all our cares, but once beheld controul;
There the poor lover that has long endur'd
Some proud Nimphs scorn, of his fond passion cur'd:

Fares

Fares like the man who firſt upon the ground
A glow-worm ſpy'd, ſuppoſing he had found
A moving Diamond, a breathing ſtone
(For life it had, and like thoſe jewels ſhone:)
He held it dear till by the ſpringing day
Inform'd, he threw the worthleſs worm away.

She ſaves the lover as we gangreen ſtay
By cutting hope like a lop't limb away:
This makes her bleeding patients to accuſe
High heaven, and theſe expoſtulations uſe:
Could nature then no private woman grace
(Whom we might dare to love) with ſuch a face,
Such a complexion, and ſo radiant eyes,
Such lovely motion, and ſuch ſharp replies?
Beyond our reach, and yet within our ſight,
What envious power has plac't this glorious light?

Thus in a ſtarry night fond children cry
For the rich ſpangles that adorn the skie,
Which though they ſhine for ever fixed there,
With light and influence relieve us here.
All her affections are to one enclin'd,
Her bounty and compaſſion to mankind:
To whom while ſhe ſo far extends her grace,
She makes but good the promiſe of her face:
For mercy has (could mercies ſelf be ſeen)
No ſweeter look then this propitious Queen;
Such guard and comfort the diſtreſſed finde
From her large power, and from her larger minde,
That whom ill fate would ruine, it prefers,
For all the miſerable are made hers.
So the fair tree whereon the Eagle builds
Poor ſheep from tempeſt, and their ſhepheard ſhields.

The

The Royall bird possesses, all the bows,
But shade and shelter to the flock allows.

Joy of our age, and safety of the next,
For which so oft thy fertile womb is vext:
Nobly contented, for the publick good
To waste thy spirits, and diffuse thy blood:
What vast hopes may these Islands entertain,
Where Monarchs thus descended are to reign?
Led by Commanders of so fair a line,
Our Seas no longer shall our power confine.

A brave Romance who would exactly frame,
First brings his Knight from some immortall Dame:
And then a weapon, and a flaming shield,
Bright as his mothers eyes he makes him weild.
None might the mother of *Achilles* be,
But the fair Pearl, and glory of the Sea.
The man to whom great *Maro* gives such fame
From the high bed of heavenly *Venus* came;
And our next *Charles*, (whom all the stars designe
Like wonders to accomplish) springs from thine.

SONG.

GO lovely Rose,
Tell her that wastes her time and me,
That now she knows
When I resemble her to thee
How sweet and fair she seems to be.

Tell

Tell her that's young,
And shuns to have her grace spy'd
That hadst thou sprung
In desarts where no men abide,
Thou must have uncommended dy'd.

Small is the worth
Of beauty from the light retir'd;
Bid her come forth,
Suffer her self to be desir'd,
And not blush so to be admir'd.

Then die that she,
The common fate of all things rare
May read in thee
How small a part of time they share,
That are so wondrous sweet and fair:

Thirsis, Galatea.

Th. AS lately I on Silver Thames did ride,
Sad *Galatea*, on the bank I spy'd:
Such was her look as sorrow taught to shine,
And thus she grac't me with a voice divine.

Gal: You that can tune your sounding strings so well
Of Ladies beauties, and of love to tell;
Once change your note, and let your Lute report
The justest grief that ever touch't the Court.

Th Fair Nimph, I have in your delights no share,
Nor ought to be concerned in your care;

Yet would I sing if I your sorrows knew,
And to my aid invoke no Muse but you.

Gal. Hear then, and let your song augment our grief
Which is so great, as not to wish relief:
She that had all which nature gives or chance,
Whom fortune joyn'd with vertue to advance,
To all the joyes this Island could afford
The greatest Mistris, and the kindest Lord:
Who with the Royal mixt her Noble blood,
And in high grace with *Gloriana* stood.
Her bounty, sweetness, beauty, goodness such,
That none ere thought her happiness too much:
So well inclin'd her favors to confer,
And kinde to all, as Heaven had been to her;
The virgins part, the mother, and the wife,
So well she acted in this span of life;
That though few years (too few alas) she told,
Shee seem'd in all things but in beauty old.
As unripe fruit, whose verdant stalks do cleave
Close to the Tree, which grieves no less to leave
The smiling pendant which adorns her so,
And until Autumn, on the Bough should grow:
So seem'd her youthful soul not easily forc't,
Or from so fair, so sweet a seat divorc't:
Her fate at once did hasty seem and slow,
At once too cruell and unwilling too.

Th. Under how hard a law are mortals born,
Whom now we engage, we anon must mourn:
What Heaven sets highest, and seems not to prize,
Is soon removed from our wondring eyes:
But since the sisters did so soon untwine
So fair a thread, I'll strive to peece the line.

Vouch-

Vouchsafe sad Nymph to let me know the Dame,
And to the Muses I'll commend her name:
Make the wide Country eccho to your moan,
The listning Trees and savage Mountains groan:
What Rocks not moved when the death is sung
Of one so good, so lovely, and so young.

Gal. 'Twas *Hamilton* whom I had nam'd before,
But naming her; grief lets me say no more.

Tabula Phœbi & Daphnis.

ARcadia juvenis Thirsis, Phœbique sacerdos,
Ingenti frustra Galateæ ardebat amore.
Haud Deus ipse olim Daphni majora canebat,
Nec fuit asperior Daphne, nec pulchrior illa:
Carminibus Phœbo dignis premit ille fugacem
Per rupes, per saxa, volans per florida vates
Pascua, formosam nunc his componere Nimpham,
Hunc illis crudelem insana mente solebat:
Audiit illa procul miserum Citheramque sonantem,
Audiit at nullis respexit mota querelis;
Ne tamen omnino caneret, desertus ad alta
Sidera perculsi, referunt nova carmina montes;
Sic non quæsitis cumulatus laudibus olim
[illegible]nsa reperit Daphni sua laurea Phœbus.

The Battel of the Summer Islands.

Cant. I.

What fruit they have, and how Heaven smiles
Upon those late discover'd Isles.

AIde me *Bellona* while the dreadful fight
Betwixt a Nation, and two Whales I write:
Seas stain'd with goar, I sing advent'rous toyl,
And how these Monsters did disarm an Isle.
Bermudas wall'd with Rocks, who does not know
That happy Island where huge Lemons grow,
And Orange Trees which golden fruit do bear,
Th'Hesperian Garden boasts of none so fair?
Where shining Pearl, Coral, and many a pound
On the rich shore, of Amber-greece is found:
The lofty Cedar which to Heaven aspires,
The Prince of Trees is fewel for their fires:
The smoak by which their loaded spits do turn
For incense, might on sacred Altars burn.
There private roofs on od'rous timber born,
Such as might Pallaces for Kings adorn:
The sweet *Palmettas*, a new *Bacchus* yield
With leaves as ample as the broadest shield:
Under the shadow of whose friendly boughs
They sit carrowsing, where their liquor grows:
Figs there unplanted through the fields do grow,
Such as fierce *Cato* did the Romans shew,
With the rare fruit inviting them to spoyl,
Carthage the mistris of so rich a soyl:
The naked rocks are not unfruitful there,
But at some constant seasons every year:

Their

Their barren top with loucious food abound,
And with the eggs of various fowls are crown'd:
Tobacco is their worst of things which they
To English Land-lords as their Tribute pay:
Such is the mould, that the blest Tenant feeds
On pretious fruits, and payes his rent in weeds:
With candid Plantines, and the jucy Pine,
On choicest Melons and sweet Grapes they dine,
And with Potato's fat their wanton Swine:
Nature these Cates with such a lavish hand
Pours out among them, that our courser Land
Tastes of that bounty, and does cloath return,
Which not for warmth, but ornament is worn:
For the kinde Spring which but salutes us here
Inhabits there, and courts them all the year:
Ripe fruits and blossoms, on the same trees live,
At once they promise what at once they give:
So sweet the air, so moderate the clime,
None sickly lives, or dies before his time.
Heaven sure has kept this spot of earth uncurst
To shew how all things were created first:
The tardy plants in our cold Orchards plac't,
Reserve their fruits for the next ages taste:
There a small grain in some few moneths will be
A firm, a lofty, and a spacious Tree:
The Parmachristi, and the fair Papah,
Now but a seed (preventing natures law)
In half the circle of the hasty year
Project a shade, and lovely fruit do wear:
And as their Trees in our dull Region set
But faintly grow, and no perfection get:
So in this Northern tract our hoarser throats
Utter unripe and ill constrained notes,
Where the supporter of the Poets stile.

Phœbus on them eternally does smile.
O how I long my carelesſ limbs to lay
Under the Plantanes ſhade, and all the day
With am'rous eyes my fancy entertain,
Invoke the Muſes, and improve my vein:
No paſſion there in my free breaſt ſhould move,
None but the ſweet and beſt of Paſſions love:
There while I ſing, if gentle love be by
That tunes my Lute, and winds the ſtrings ſo high:
With the ſweet ſound of *Sachariſſa*'s name,
I'll make the liſtning ſalvages grow tame.
 But while I do theſe pleaſing dreams indite,
 I am diverted from the promis'd fight.

Canto II.

Of their affright, and how their foes
Diſcovered were, this Canto ſhews.

THough Rocks ſo high about this Iland riſe,
 That well they may the num'rous Turk deſpiſe;
Yet is no humane fate exempt from fear (hear
Which ſhakes their hearts, while through the Ile they
A laſting noiſe, as horrid and as loud
As thunder makes before it breaks the cloud.
Three days they dread this murmur ere they know
From what blind cauſe th'unwonted ſound may grow:
At length two Monſters of unequal ſize
Hard by the ſhore a fiſher man eſpies;
Two mighty Whales, which ſwellings Seas had toſt,
And left them priſoners on the rocky coaſt;
One as a Mountain vaſt, and with her came
A Cub not much inferior to his Dam:

Here

Here in a pool among the Rocks ingag'd,
They roar'd like Lions caught in toyls and rag'd:
The man knew what they were, who heretofore
Had seen the like lye murdered on the shore,
By the wild fury of some tempest cast
The fate of ships and shipwrackt men to taste;
As carelesse dames whom wine and sleep betray
To frantick dreams their Infants overlay:
So there sometime the raging Ocean fails,
And her own brood exposes when the Whales
Against sharp Rocks like reeling vessels quash't,
Though huge as Mountains, are in peeces dash't;
Along the shore their dreadful limbs lie scatter'd,
Like Hills with Earthquakes shaken, torn and shatter'd:
Heart sure of brass they had who tempted first,
Rude Seas that spare not what themselves have nurst.
  The welcome news through all the Nation spread,
  To sudden joy and hope converts their dread.
What lately was their publick terror, they
Behold with glad eyes as a certain prey;
Dispose already of th'untaken spoil,
And as if purchase of their future toyl,
These share the bones, and they divide the oyl;
So was the Huntsman by the Bear opprest,
Whose hide he sold before he caught the beast.

  They man their Boats, and all their young men arm
With whatsoever may the Monsters harm;
Pikes, Holberts, Spits and Darts, that wound so far
The Tools of Peace, and Instruments of War:
Now was the time for vigrous lads to shew
What love or honor could invite them too;
A goodly Theatre where Rocks are round
With reverend age, and lovely lasses crown'd:

Such was the lake which held this dreadful pare
Within the bounds of noble *Warwicks* share:
WarWicks bold Earl, then which no title bears
A greater sound among our British Peers;
And worthy he the memory to renew
The fate and honor, to that title due;
Whose brave adventures have transfer'd his name,
And through the new world spread his growing fame.
 But how they fought, and what their valour gain'd,
 Shall in another Canto be contain'd.

Canto III.

The bloody fight, successless toyl,
And how the Fish sack'd the Isle.

THe Boat which on the first assault did go
 Stroke with a harping Iron the younger fo;
Who when he felt his side so rudely goar'd
Loud as the Seas that nourish't him he roar'd;
As a broad bream to please some curious taste,
While yet alive in boyling water cast;
Vex't w th unwonted heat, boyls, flings about
The scorching brass, and hurls the liquor out:
So with the barbed Javeling stung, he raves,
And scourges with his tayl the suffering waves:
Like fairy *Talas* with his iron flayl,
He threatens ruine with his pondrous tayl;
Dissolving at one stroke the battered Boat,
And down the men fall drenched in the Moat:
With every fierce encounter they are forc't
To quit their Boats, and fare like men unhorst.

The

The bigger Whale like some huge Carrack lay,
Which wanteth Sea room, with her foes to play;
Slowly she swims, and when provok'd she wo'd
Advance her tail, her head salutes the mud.
The shallow water doth her force infringe,
And renders vain her tails impetuous swinge.
The shining steel her tender sides receive,
And there like Bees they all their weapons leave.
This sees the Cub, and does himself oppose
Betwixt his cumbred mother and her foes:
With desperate courage he receives her wounds,
And men and boats his active tayl confounds.
Their Surges joyn'd, the Seas with billows fill,
And make a tempest, though the winds be still.
Now would the men with half their hoped prey
Be well content, and wish this cub away:
Their wish they have, he to direct his dam
Unto the gap through which they thither came,
Before her swims, and quits the hostile lake,
A pris'ner there, but for his mothers sake:
She by the Rocks compell'd to stay behind,
Is by the vastness of her bulks confin'd,
They shout for joy, and now on her alone
Their fury falls, and all their darts are thrown:
Their Lances spent; one bolder then the rest
With his broad sword provok'd the sluggish beast:
Her oily side devours blade and heft,
And there his Steel the bold Bermudian left.
Courage the rest from his example take,
And now they change the colour of the lake:
Blood flows in Rivers from her wounded side,
As if they would prevent the tardy tide;
And raise the flood to that propitious height,
As might convey her from this fatal streight.

She swims in blood, and blood do's spouting throw
To Heaven, that Heaven mens cruelties might know.
Their fixed Javelings in her side she wears,
And on her back a grove of pikes appears.
You would have thought had you the monster seen
Thus drest, she had another Island been:
Roaring she tears the air with such noise,
(As well resembled with conspiring voice
Of routed Armies, when the field is won)
To reach the ears of her escaped son.
He (though a league escaped from the fo)
Hastes to her aid, the pious Trojan so
Neglecting for *Creusas* life his own,
Repeats the danger of the burning Town,
The men amazed blush to see the seed
Of monsters, humane piety exceed,
Well proves this kindness what the Grecians sung,
That loves bright mother from the Ocean sprung.
Their courage droops, and hopeless now they wish
For composition with th'unconquer'd fish:
So she their weapons would restore again,
Through rocks they'd hew her passage to the main.
But how instructed in each others minde,
Or what commerce can men with monsters finde:
Not daring to approach their wounded fo,
Whom her couragious son protected so:
They charge their Musket, and with hot desire
Of fell revenge, renew the fight with fire.
Standing alooff with lead, they bruise the scales,
And tare the flesh of the incensed Whales.
But no success their fierce endeavors found,
Nor this way could they give one fatall wound.
Now to their Fort they are about to send
For the loud Engines which their Isle defend.

But

But what those pieces fram'd to batter walls
Would have effected on those mighty Whales,
Great *Neptune* will not have us know, who findes
A tyde so high, that it relieves his friends.
And thus they parted with exchange of harms,
Much blood the Monsters lost, and they their Arms.

Upon the death of my Lady Rich.

MAy those already curst *Essexian* plains,
Where hasty death and pining sickness raigns,
Prove all a Desart, and none there make stay,
But savage Beasts, or men as ill as they.
There the fair light which all our Island grac'd,
Like *Hero's* taper in the windows plac'd;
Such fate from the malignant air did find,
As that exposed to the boystrous wind.
Ah cruel Heaven to snatch so soon away
Her, for whose life had we had time to pray,
With thousand vows and tears we should have sought,
That sad decrees suspension to have wrought.
But we (alas) no whisper of her pain,
Heard till 'twas sin to wish her here again.
That horrid word at once like lightning spread,
Strook all our ears, The Lady *Rich* is dead.
Heart rending news, and dreadful to those few
Who her resemble, and her steps pursue.
That death should licence have to rage among
The fair, the wise, the vertuous, and the young.
The *Paphian* Queen from that fierce battell born,
With goared hand and vail so rudely torn:

Like

Like terror did among th'immortals breed,
Taught by her wound that Godesses might bleed:
All stand amazed, but beyond the rest
Th'heroique Dame whose happy womb she blest,
Mov'd with just grief expostulates with Heaven,
Urging that promise to th'obsequious given,
Of longer life, for nere was pious soul
More apt t'obey, more worthy to controul:
A skilful eye at once, might read the race
Of Caledonian Monarchs in her face;
And sweet humility her look and minde,
At once were lofty, and at once were kinde.
There dwelt the scorn of vice, and pity too,
For those that did what she disdain'd to do:
So gentle and severe, that what was bad
At once her hatred and her pardon had.
Gracious to all, but where her love was due,
So fast, so faithful, loyal and so true,
That a bold hand as soon might hope to force
The rouling lights of Heaven, as change her course.
  Some happy Angel that beholds her there,
Instruct us to record what she was here:
And when this cloud of sorrow's over-blown,
Through the wide world weel make her graces known;
So fresh the wound is, and the grief so vast,
That all our art and power of speech is waste.
Here passion swayes, but there the Muse shall raise
Eternal monuments of louder praise.
  There our delight complying with her fame,
Shall have occasion to recite thy name,
Fair *Sacharissa*, and now onely fair,
To sacred friendship weel an Altar rear:
Such as the Romans did erect of old,
Where on a marble pillar shall be told

The

The lovely passion each to other bare,
With the resemblance of that matchless pair,
Narcissus to the thing for which he pin'd,
Was not more like then yours to her fair mind:
Save that you grac'd the several part of life,
A spotle's Virgin, and a faultless wife.
Such was the sweet converse 'twixt her and you,
As that she holds with her associates now.
How false is hope, and how regardless fate,
That such a love should have so short a date?
Lately I saw her sighing, part from thee
(Alas that that the last farewel should be!)
So look't *Astrea*, her remove design'd
On those distressed friends she left behind:
Consent in vertue, knit your heart so fast,
That still the knot in spight of death does last:
For as your tears and sorrow-wounded soul
Prove well that on your part this bond is whole.
So all we know of what they do above,
Is, that they happy are, and that they love;
Let dark oblivion, and the hollow grave
Content themselves our frailer thoughts to have:
Well chosen love is never taught to die,
But with our nobler part invades the skie:
Then grieve no more, that one so heavenly shap'd
The crooked hand of trembling age escap'd;
Rather since we beheld her not decay,
But that she vanish'd so entire away.
Her wondrous beauty and her goodness merit,
We should suppose that some propitious spirit,
In that celestial form frequented here,
And is not dead, but ceases to appear.

To the Queen-Mother upon her Landing.

GReat *Queen* of *Europe* where thy off-spring wears
All the chief Crowns, whose Princes are thy heirs,
As welcome thou to Sea, girt *Brittains* shore,
As erst *Latona* (who fair *Cinthia* bore)
To *Delos* was. Here shines a Nimph as bright,
By thee disclos'd, with like increase of light.
Why was her joy in *Belgia* confin'd ?
Or why did you so much regard the wind ?
Scarce could the Ocean (though inrag'd) have tost
Thy Soveraign bark; but where th'obsequious coast
Pay tribute to thy bed: *Romes* conquering hand
More vanquish'd Nations under her command,
Never reduc'd; glad *Berecinthia*, so
Among her deathless Progeny did go,
A wreath of Towers adorn'd her reverend head,
Mother of all that on *Ambrosia* fed:
Thy godly race must sway the age to come,
As she *Olympus*, peopled with her womb,
Would those Commanders of mankinde obey
Their honored Parent, all pretences lay
Down at your Royal feet, compose the jars,
And on the growing Turk discharge these wars:
The Christian Knights that sacred tomb should wrest,
From Pagan hands, and triumph o'r the East.
The *Englands* Princes, and *Gallia's* Dolphin might
Like young *Rinaldo*, and *Tancredo* fight
In single combate; by their swords again
The proud *Argantes*, and fierce *Soldans* slain.
Again, might we their deeds recite,
And with your *Thuscan* exalt the fight.

Song.

SONG.

PEace babling Muse,
I dare not sing what you indite :
Her eyes refuse
To read the passion which they write.
She strikes my Lute, but if it sound,
Threatens to hurl it on the ground.
And I no less her anger dread,
Then the poor wretch that fains him dead:
While some fierce Lion does embrace
His breathless corps, and lick his face.
Wrap't up in silent fears he lies,
Torn all in pieces if he cries.

Of Love.

ANger in hasty words or blows,
It self discharges on our foes.
And sorrow too, findes some relief,
In tears which wait upon our grief.
So every passion, but fond love,
Unto its own redress does move.
But that alone the wretch inclines
To what prevents his own designs :
Makes him lament, and sigh, and weep,
Disordred, tremble, fawn and creep,
Postures which render him despis'd,
Where he endeavors to be priz'd.

For

For women born to be controul'd
Stoop to the forwards and the bold,
Affect the haughty and the proud,
The gay and frollick, and the loud;
Who first the gen'rous steed opprest,
Not kneeling did salute the beast;
But with high courage life and force
Approaching, tam'd th'unruly horse.
Unwisely we, the wiser East
Pity supposing them opprest
With Tyrants force whose law is will,
By which they govern, spoil and kill
Each Nimph, but moderately fair,
Command with no less rigor here.
  Should some brave Turk that walks among
His twenty Lasses bright and young,
And beckens to the willing Dame
Preferr'd to quench his present flame:
Behold as many Gallants here,
With modest guise, and silent fear,
All to our Female Idol bend,
Whilest her high pride does scarce descend.
To mark their follies he would swear
That these her guard of Eunuchs were;
And that a more Majestique Queen,
Or humbler slaves he had not seen.
  All this with indignation spoke,
In vain I strugled with the yoke
Of mighty love, that conquering look,
When next beheld like lightning stroke
My blasted soul, and made me bow
Lower then those I pitied now.
  So the tall Stag upon the brink
Of some smooth stream about to drink,

Surveying

Surveying there his armed head,
With shame remembers that he fled.
The scorned dogs resolves to try
The combates next, but if their cry
Invades again his trembling ear,
He straight resumes his wonted fear:
Leaves the untasted Spring behind,
And wing'd with fear, out-flies the wind:

To the mutable Fair.

HEre *Cœlia* for thy sake I part
With all that grew so neer my heart:
The Passion that I had for thee,
The Faith, the Love, the Constancy,
And that I may successful prove,
Transform my self to what you love.
  Fool that I was so much to prize
Those simple vertues you despise.
Fool that with such dull arrows strove,
Or hop'd to reach a flying Dove.
For you that are in motion still,
Decline our force, and mock our skill.
Who like Don *Quixot* do advance
Against a Wind-mill our vain launce.
  Now will I wander through the air,
Mount make a stoop at every fair,
And with a fancy unconfin'd
(As lawless as the Sea or wind)
Pursue you wheresoe'er you flie,
And with your various thoughts comply.

The formal ſtars do travel ſo,
As we their names and courſes know,
And he that on their changes looks,
Would think they govern'd by our books.
But never were the clouds reduc'd
To any Art, the motion us'd:
By thoſe free vapors are ſo light,
So frequent, that the conquer'd ſight
Deſpair to finde the rules that guide
Thoſe gilded ſhadows as they ſlide.
And therefore of the ſpacious air
Joves royal conſort had the care:
And by that power did once eſcape,
Declining bold *Ixions* rape.
She with her own reſemblance grac'd,
A ſhining cloud which he embrac'd.
Such was that Image ſo it ſmil'd,
With ſeeming kindneſs which beguil'd
Your *Thirſis* lately when he thought
He had his fleeting *Cœlia* caught.
'Twas ſhap'd like her, but for the fair
He fill'd his arms with yeelding air.
A fate for which he grieves the leſs,
Becauſe the gods had like ſucceſs.
For in their ſtory one (we ſee)
Purſues a Nimph, and takes a Tree:
A ſecond with a Lovers haſte
Soon overtakes whom he had chac't.
But ſhe that did a virgin ſeem
Poſſeſt, appears a wandring ſtream.
For his ſuppoſed love a third
Layes greedy hold upon a bird:
And ſtands amaz'd to finde his dear,
A wilde inhabitant of th'air.

To

To these old tales such Nimphs as you
Give credit, and still make them new.
The Am'rous now like wonders finde
In the swift changes of your minde.
But *Cœlia* if you apprehend
The Muse of your incensed friend:
Nor would that he record your blame,
And make it live repeat the same.
Again deceive him and again,
And then he swears he'll not complain.
For still to be deluded so,
Is all the pleasures Lovers know:
Who, like good Faulkners take delight,
Not in the quarrey, but the flight.

Of Salley.

OF *Jason*, *Theseus*, and such worthies old,
Light seem the tales antiquity has told.
Such beasts and monsters as their force opprest
Some places onely, and sometimes infest.
Salley that scorn'd all power and laws of men,
Goods with their owners hurrying to their den.
And future ages threatning with a rude
And savage race successively renew'd.
Their King despising with rebellious pride,
And foes profest to all the world beside,
This pest of mankinde gives our *Hero* fame,
And through th'obliged world dilates his name.
The Prophet once to cruel *Agag* said,
As thy fierce sword has mothers childless made:

So shall the sword make thine ; and with that word
He hew'd the man in peece with his sword.
Just *Charles* like measure has return'd to these,
Whose Pagan hands had stain'd the troubled Seas ;
With ships they made the spoiled Merchant mourn,
With ships their City and themselves are torn.
One squadron of our winged Castles sent
O'r-threw their Fort, and all their Navy rent:
For not content the dangers to encrease,
And act the part of tempest in the Seas,
Like hungry Woolves these pirates from our shore,
Whole flocks of sheep, and ravish'd cattell bore.
Safely they did on other Nations prey,
Fools to provoke the Soveraign of the Sea.
Mad *Cacus* so whom like ill fate perswades
The heard of fair *Alcmena*'s seed invades.
Who for revenge, and mortals glad relief,
Sack'd the dark cave, and crush'd that horrid theif.
Moroccos Monarch wondring at this fact,
Save that his presence his affairs exact,
Had come in person to have seen and known
The injur'd worlds revenger, and his own.
Hither he sends the chief among his Peers,
Who in his Bark well chosen presents bears
To the renown'd for piety and force,
Poor captives manumiz'd and matchless horse.

To Mrs. Braughton.

FAir fellow servant may your gentle ear
Prove more propitious to my sleighted care :

Then

Then the bright Dames we serve, for her relief,
(Vext with the long expressions of my grief)
Receive these plaints, nor will her high disdain
Forbid my humble Muse to court her train.
So in those Nations which the Sun adore,
Some modest *Persian*, or some weak ey'd *More*,
No higher dares advance his dazled sight
Then to some gilded cloud, which neer the light
Of their ascending God adorns the East,
And graced with his beams out-shines the rest.
Thy skilfull hand contributes to our wo,
And whets those arrows which confounds us so:
A thousand *Cupids* in those curls do sit,
Those curious nets those slender fingers knit.
The graces put not more exactly on
Th'attire of *Venus*, when the Ball she won,
Then *Sacharissa* by thy care is drest,
When all our youth prefers her to the rest.
You the soft seasons know when best her minde
May be to pity or to love enclin'd,
In some well chosen hour supply his fear,
Whose hopeless love durst never tempt the ear
Of that stern goddess you (her Priest) declare
What offerings may propitiate the fair
Rich orient Pearl, bright stones that ne'er decay,
Or pollisht lines which longer last then they.
For if I thought she took delight in those,
To where the cheerful morn does first disclose,
(The shady night removing of her beams)
Wing'd with bold love, I'd flie to fetch such gems:
But since her eyes, her teeth, her lip excells
All that is found in mines, or fishes shells:
Her nobler part as far exceeding these,
None but immortal gifts her minde can please.

Those shining Jewels *Greece* and *Troy* bestow'd,
The snowy wrists and lovely neck did load,
Of *Sparta*'s Queen. But when the Town was burn'd,
Those fading glories were to ashes turn'd:
Her beauty too had perish'd, and her fame,
Had not the muse redeem'd them from the flame.

Puerperium.

YOu Gods that have the power,
To trouble, and compose
All that's beneath your bower,
Calm silence on the Seas, on Earth impose.

Fair *Venus* in thy soft arms,
The God of rage confine,
For thy whispers are the charms
Which onely can divert his fierce design.

What though he frown, and to tumults do incline,
Thou the flame,
Kindled in his breast can'st tame,
With that snow which unmelted lies on thine?

Great Goddess give this thy sacred Island rest,
Make Heaven smile,
That no storm disturb us, while
Thy chief care our *Halcyon* builds her nest.

Great *Gloriana*; fair *Gloriana*,
Bright as high Heaven is, and fertile as Earth,

Whose

Whose beauty relieves us,
Whose Royal bed gives us
Both glory and peace.
Our present joy, and our hopes increase.

To Phillis.

P*Hillis*, why should we delay
Pleasures shorter then the day?
Could we (which we never can)
Stretch our lives beyond their span?
Beauty like a shadow flies,
And our youth before us dies,
Or would youth and beauty stay,
Love hath wings, and will away.
Love hath swifter wings then time;
Change in love to Heaven does clime.
Gods that never change their state,
Varied oft their love and hate.
Phillis, to this truth we ow,
All the love betwixt us two:
Let not you and I inquire,
What has been our past desire,
On what Shepherds you have smil'd,
Or what Nimphs I have beguil'd.
Leave it to the Planets too,
What we shall hereafter do:
For the joys we now may prove,
Take advice of present love.

To Phillis.

P*Hillis*, 'twas love that injur'd you,
And on that Rock your *Thirsis* threw,
Who for proud *Cœlia* could have dy'd,
Whilst you no less accus'd his pride.
Fond Love his darts at random throws,
And nothing springs from what he sows,
From foes discharg'd as often meet,
The shining points of arrows fleet,
In the wide air creating fire,
As souls that joyn in one desire.
Love made the lovely *Venus* burn
In vain, and for the cold youth mourn:
Who the pursuit of churlish Beasts,
Preferr'd to sleeping on her Brests.
Love makes so many hearts the prize,
Of the bright *Carliles* conquering eyes,
Which she regards no more then they,
The tears of lesser beauties weigh.
So have I seen the lost clouds pour,
Into the Sea a useless shower,
And the vext Sailors curse the rain,
For which poor shepherds pray'd in vain.
Then *Phillis*, since our passions are
Govern'd by chance, and not the care
But sport of Heaven which takes delight
To look upon this *Parthian* flight
Of Love, still flying or in chase,
Never incountring face to face.
No more to love weel sacrifice,
But to the best of Deities:

And

And let our hearts which love disjoyn'd,
By his kind Mother be combin'd.

SONG.

VV Hile I liſten to thy voice,
Chloris, I feel my life decay,
That powerful noiſe
Calls my flitting ſoul away.
Oh ſuppreſs that Magick ſound,
Which deſtroyes without a wound!

Peace *Chloris* peace, or ſinging die,
That together you and I,
To Heaven may go,
For all we know:
Of what the bleſſed do above
Is that they ſing, and that they love.

SONG.

STay *Phœbus*, ſtay,
The world to which you flie ſo faſt:
Conveying day,
From us to them can pay your haſt,
With no ſuch object, nor ſalute your riſe
With no ſuch wonder, as *de Mornay*'s eyes.

Well

Well do this prove,
The error of those Antique books,
Which made you move,
About the world her charming looks
Would fix your beams, and make it ever day,
Did not the rowling Earth snatch her away.

To Amoret.

A*Moret*, thy milky way,
Fram'd of many nameless stars,
The smooth stream where none can say,
He this drop to that prefers.

Amoret, my lovely fo,
Tell me where thy strength does lie,
Where the power that charms us so,
In thy Soul, or in thy eye?

By that snowy neck alone,
Or thy grace in motion seen,
No such wonders could be done:
Yet thy wa[illegible]e is streight and clean,
As *Cupids* shaft, or *Hermes* rod,
And powerful too, as either God.

To my Lord of Falkland.

BRave *Holland* lead, and with him *Falkland* goes,
Who hears this told, and does not streight suppose
We send the Graces and the Muses forth,
To civilize, and to instruct the North ?
Not that these Ornaments make swords less sharp,
Apollo wears as well his Bow as Harp ;
And though he be the Patron of that Spring,
Where in calm peace, the sacred Virgins sing.
He courage had to guard th'invaded throne
Of Love, and cast th'ambitious Giants down.
Ah (noble Friend) with what impatience all
That know thy worth, and know how prodigal
Of thy great Soul thou art, longing to twist
Bayes with that Ivy, which so early kist
Thy youthful Temples ? with what horror we
Think on the blind events of war and thee ?
To Fate exposing that all-knowing brest,
Among the throng as cheaply as the rest :
Where Oaks and Brambles (if the copse be burn'd)
Confounded lie to the same ashes turn'd.
Some happy wind over the Ocean blow
This tempest yet, which frights our Island so.
Guarded with ships, and all the Sea our own,
From Heaven this mischief on our heads is thrown.
In a late dream the *genius* of this Land,
Amaz'd, I saw, like a fair Hebrew stand,
When first she felt the twins begin to jar,
And found her womb the seat of Civil war :
Inclin'd to whose relief, and with presage
Of better fortune for the present age,

Heaven

Heaven send's, quoth I, this discord for our good,
To warm, perhaps, but not to waste our blood,
To raise our drooping spirits, grown the scorn
Of our proud neighbors, who ere long shall mourn,
(Though now they joy in our expected harms)
We had occasion to resume our Arms.
 A Lyon so with self-provoking smart,
His rebel tail scourging his nobler part,
Calls up his courage, then begins to roar,
And charge his foes, who thought him mad before.

Of a Lady who writ in praise of Mira.

WHile she pretends to make the Graces known,
 Of matchless *Mira*, she reveals her own,
And when she would anothers praise indite,
Is by her glass instructed how to write.

To one married to an old Man.

SInce thou wouldst needs, betwitcht with some ill
Be buried in those monumental arms: (charms,
All we can wish, is, may that earth lie light
Upon the tender limbs, and so good night.

For drinking of Healths.

LEt Bruits, and Vegetals that cannot think,
So far as drought and nature urges drink:
A more indulgent Mistress guides our sprights,
Reason, that dares beyond our appetites,
She would our care as well as thirst redress,
And with Divinity rewards excess.
Deserted *Ariadne* thus supply'd,
Did perjur'd *Theseus* cruelty deride,
Bacchus imbrac'd from her exalted thought,
Banish'd the man, her passion, and his fault.
Bacckus and *Phœbus* are by *Jove* ally'd,
And each by others timely heat supply'd:
All that the Grapes ow to his lightning fires,
Is paid in numbers which their juyce inspires.
Wine fills the veins, and healths are understood,
To give our Friends a title to our Blood:
Who naming me, doth warm his courage so,
Shews for my sake what his bold hand would do.

To Flavia, *Song:*

TIs not your beauty can ingage
My wary heart:
The Sun in all his pride and rage,
Has not that Art:
And yet he shines as bright as you,
If brightness could our souls subdue.

'Tis

'Tis not the pretty things you say,
Nor those you write,
Which can make *Thirsis* heart your prey,
For that delight:
The graces of a well-taught minde,
In some of our own we finde.

No *Flavia*, 'tis your love, I fear
Loves surest darts,
Those which so seldom fail him are
Headed with hearts.
Their very shadows make us yeeld,
Dissemble well, and win the field.

On my Lady Isabella *playing on the Lute.*

SUch moving sounds, from such a careless touch,
So unconcern'd her self, and we so much:
What Art is this, that with so little pains,
Transports us thus, and o'r the spirit reigns?
The trembling strings above her fingers proud,
And tell their joy for every kiss aloud:
Small force there needs to make thee tremble so,
Touch't by that hand; who would not tremble tro?
Here Love takes stand, and while she charms the ear
Empties his quiver on the listning Deer:
Musick so softens and disarms the minde,
That not an Arrow does resistance finde.
Thus the fair tyrant celebrates the prize,
And acts her self the triumph of her eyes.

So

So *Nero* once with Harp in hand, ſurvay'd
His flaming *Rome*, and as it burnt he play'd.

The Fall.

SEe how the will-earth gives way
To take th'impreſſion where ſhe lay:
See how the mould as loath to leave
So ſweet a burden, ſtill doth cleave
Cloſe to the Nimphs ſtain'd garment? here
The coming Spring would firſt appear,
And all this place with Roſes ſtrow,
If buſie feet would let them grow.
Here *Venus* ſmil'd to ſee blinde Chance
It ſelf, before her ſon advance,
And a fair image to preſent
Of what the Boy ſo long had meant:
'Twas ſuch a chance as this made all
The World into this order fall:
Thus the firſt lovers, on the clay
Of which they were compoſed lay;
So in their prime with equal grace
Met the firſt patterns of our race:
Then bluſh not (fair) or on him frown,
Or wonder how you both came down;
But touch him, and he'll tremble ſtrait,
How could he then ſupport your weight?
How could the Youth alas, but bend
When his whole Heaven upon him lean'd?
If ought by him amiſs were done,
'Twas that he let you riſe ſo ſoon.

Of Silvia.

OUr fighs are heard, juſt Heav'n declares
The ſenſe it has of lovers cares;
She that ſo far the reſt out-ſhin'd,
Silvia the fair whiles ſhe was kinde;
As if her frowns impair'd her brow,
Seems onely not unhandſome now:
 So when the sky makes us endure
 A ſtorm, it ſelf becomes obſcure.

Hence 'tis that I conceal my flame,
Hiding from *Flavia*'s ſelf her name;
Leſt ſhe provoking Heaven ſhould prove
How it rewards neglected love;
Better a thouſand ſuch as I
Their grief untold ſhould pine and die:
 Then her bright morning over-caſt
 With ſullen clouds ſhould be defac't.

The Budd.

LAtely on yonder ſwelling buſh,
Big with many a comming Roſe,
This early Bud began to bluſh,
And did but half it ſelf diſcloſe;
 And pluck't it, though no better grown,
 Yet now you ſee how full 'tis blown.

Still

Still as I did the leaves inspire,
With such a purple light they shon
As if they had been made of fire,
And spreading so, would flame anon:
  All that was meant by Air or Sun
  To the young flower my breath has done.

If our loose breath so much can do,
What may the same inform's of love,
Of purest love and musick too
When *Flavia* it aspires to move:
  When that which life-less buds perswades
  To wax more soft her youth invades.

To a Lady singing a Song of his composing.

CHloris your self you so excel
When you vouchsafe to breath my thought,
That like a spirit with this spell
Of my own teaching I am taught.

That Eagles fate and mine are one
Which on that shaft that made him die,
Espy'd a feather of his own
Wherewith he meant to soar so high:

Had eccho with so sweet a grace,
Narcissus loud complaints return'd,
Not for reflexion of his face;
But of his voice the Boy had mourn'd.

At the marriage of the Dwarfs.

THe sign or chance makes others wive,
But nature did this match contrive;
Eve might as well have *Adam* fled
As she deny'd her little Bed
To him for whom Heaven seem'd to frame,
And measure out this onely dame.

Thrice happy is that humble pair
Beneath the level of all care;
Over whose heads those arrows flie
Of sad distrust and jealousie:
Secur'd in as high extream,
As if the world held none but them:

To him the fairest Nymphs do shew
Like moving mountains top't with snow:
And every Man a Polipheme
Does to his *Galatea* seem:
None may presume her faith to prove,
He proffers death that proffers love.

Ah (*Chloris*) that kinde nature thus
From all the world had sever'd us:
Creating for our selves us two,
As love has me for onely you.

Upon

Upon Ben. Johnson.

MIrror of Poets, mirror of our age!
Which her whole face beholding on thy stage;
Pleas'd and displeas'd with her own faults, indures
A remedy like those whom musick cures:
Thou hast alone those various inclinations
Which Nature gives to Ages, Sexes, Nations;
Hast tracked with thy All-resembling Pen
What ever custom has impos'd on men:
Or ill got habit which deserts them so,
That scarce one Brother can the Brother know,
Is representing to the wondring eyes
Of all that see or read thy Comedies:
Who ever in those Glasses look, may finde
The spots return'd, or graces of the minde:
And by the help of so divine an Art
At leisure view and dress his nobler part.
Narcissus couzened by that flatt'ring Well,
And nothing could but of his beauty tell,
Had here discovering that the deform'd estate
Of his fond minde preserv'd himself with hate;
But Vertue too as well as Vice, is clad
In Flesh and Blood so well, that *Plato* had
Beheld what his high fancy once embrac't,
Vertue with colours, speech, and motion grac't:
The sundry postures of thy copious muse,
Who would express a thousand Tongues must use;
Whose fate's no less peculiar then thy Art,
For as thou couldst all characters impart:
So none could render thine who still escapes
Like *Proteus* in variety of shapes:

Who was, nor this, nor that, but all we finde,
And all we can imagine in mankinde.

To Mr. George Sands, *on his Translation of some parts of the Bible.*

HOw bold a work attempts that pen,
Which would inrich our vulgar tongue
With the high raptures of those men,
Who here with the same spirit sung,
  Wherewith they now assist the Quire
  Of Angels, who their Songs admire?

What-ever those inspired Souls
Were urged to express did shake,
The aged deep, and both the Poles
Their num'rous Thunder could awake
  Dull Earth, which does with Heaven consent,
  To all they wrote, and all they meant.

Say (Sacred Bard) what could bestow
Courage on thee, to soar so high?
Tell me (brave Friend) what help'd thee so
To shake off all mortality?
  To light this Torch, thou hast climb'd higher,
  Then he who stole Celestial fire.

Chloris

Chloris *and* Hilas.

Chl. HIlas, ô *Hilas*, why ſit we mute,
Now that each Bird ſaluteth the Spring ;
Winde up the ſlackned ſtrings of thy Lute,
Never canſt thou want matter to ſing ?
For love thy Breſt does fill with a ſuch a fire,
That whatſo'er is fair, moves thy deſire.

Hil. Sweeteſt you know, the ſweeteſt of things,
Of various flowers the Bees do compoſe,
Yet no particular taſte it brings
Of Violet, Woodbind, Pink, or Roſe :
So love the reſultance is of all our graces
Which flow from a thouſand ſeveral faces.

Chl. *Hilas*, the Birds which chant in this Grove,
Could we but know their Language they uſe,
They would inſtruct us better in love,
And reprehend thy inconſtant muſe :
For love their Breſts does fill with ſuch a fire,
That what they once do chuſe, bounds their deſire.

Hil. *Chloris* this change the Birds do approve,
Which the warm ſeaſon hither does bring ;
Times from your ſelf does further remove
You, then the Winter from the gay Spring :
She that like lightning ſhin'd while her face laſted,
The Oak now reſembles which lightning have blaſted.

Under a Ladies Picture.

SUch *Hellen* was, and who can blame the Boy
That in so bright a flame consum'd his Troy?
But had like vertue shin'd in that fair Greek,
The am'rous shepherd had not dar'd to seek,
Or hope for pity, but with silent moan;
And better fate had perished all alone.

In answer of Sir John Suckling'*s Verses.*

Con.

STay here fond youth, and ask no more, be wise,
Knowing too much, long since lost Paradise.

Pro.

And by your knowledge we should be bereft
Of all that Paradise which yet is left.

Con:

The vertuous joyes thou hast, thou wouldst, should still
Last in their pride, and wouldst not take it ill:
If rudely from sweet dreams, and for a toy
Thou awak't, he wakes himself that does enjoy.

Pro.

How can the joy or hope which you allow
Be stiled vertuous, and the end not so?
Talk in your sleep, and shadows still admire.
'Tis true, he wakes that feels this real fire,
But to sleep better; for who ere drinks deep
Of this *Nepenthe*, rocks himself asleep.

Con

Con.

Fruition adds no new wealth, but deſtroyes,
And while it pleaſeth much, yet ſtill it cloyes:
Who thinks he ſhall be happier made for that,
As reaſonably might hope he might grow fat
By eating to a ſurfeit, this once paſt,
What reliſhes? even kiſſes loſe their taſte.

Pro.

Bleſſings may be repeated, while they cloy,
But ſhall we ſtarve, cauſe ſurfeiting deſtroy?
And if fruition did the taſte impair
Of kiſſes; why ſhould yonder happy pair
Where joyes, juſt Himen, warrants all the night
Conſume the day too in this leſs delight.

Con:

Urge not 'tis neceſſary; alas we know
The homelieſt thing that mankinde does, is ſo.
The world is of a large extent we ſee,
And muſt be peopled, children there muſt be,
So muſt bread too, but ſince there are enough
Born to that drudgery, what need we plough.

Pro.

I need not plough ſince what the ſtooping Hinde
Gets of my pregnant Land, muſt all be mine:
But in this nobler tillage 'tis not ſo;
For when *Anchiſes* did fair *Venus* know
What intreſt had poor Vulcan in the Boy,
Great bold *Æneas*, or the preſent joy.

Con.

Women enjoy'd what 'eretofore they have been,
Are like Romances read, or Scenes once ſeen:
Fruition dulls, or ſpoils the play much more
Then if one read, or knew the plot before.

Pro.

Playes and Romances read, and ſeen, do fall
In our opinions, yet not ſeen at all:
Whom would they pleaſe? to an Heroick tale,
Would you not liſten, leſt it ſhould grow ſtale?

Con.

'Tis expectation makes a bleſſing dear,
Heaven were not Heaven, if we knew what it were.

Pro.

If 'twere not Heaven, if we knew what it were,
'Twould not be Heaven to thoſe that now are there.

Con.

As in proſpects, we are there pleaſed moſt,
Where ſomething keeps the eye from being loſt,
And leaves room to gueſs; ſo here reſtraint,
Holds up delight, that with exceſs would faint.

Pro.

Reſtraint preſerves the pleaſure we have got,
But he ne'r has it, that injoys it not.
In goodly proſpects who contracts the ſpace,
Or takes not all the bounty of the place?
We wiſh remov'd what ſtandeth in our light,
And nature blam'd for limiting our ſight,
Where you ſtand wiſely winking at the view
Of the fair proſpect, may be always new.

Con.

They who know all the wealth they have, are poor:
He's onely rich that cannot tell his ſtore.

Pro.

Not he that knows the wealth he has, is poor,
But he that dares not touch, nor uſe his ſtore.

To A. H. *of the different success of their Loves.*

THrice happy pair of whom we cannot know,
Which first began to love, or loves most now :
Fair course of passion where two lovers start,
And run together, heart still yoak't in heart :
Succesful youth, whom love has taught the way,
To be victorious in thy first essay.
Sure love's an Art best practised at first.
And where th'experienc'd still prosper worst.
I with a different fate pursu'd in vain
The haughty *Cœlia*, till my just disdain
Of her neglect, above that passion born,
Did pride to pride oppose, and scorn to scorn,
Now she relents, but all too late to move
A heart directed to a Nobler love :
The scales are turn'd, her Kingdom weighs no more,
Now, then my vows and service did before :
So in some well wrought hangings you may see
How *Hector* leads, and how the *Grecians* fly;
Here the fierce *Mars* his courage so inspires;
That with bold hands the *Argive* Fleet he fires,
But there from Heaven the blew ey'd Virgin falls,
And frighted *Troy* retires within her Walls.
They that are foremost in that bloody place,
Turn head anon, and gives the Couqu'rors chace;
So like the chances are of Love and War,
That they alone in this distinguish'd are :
In love the Victors from the vanquish'd flie,
They flie that wound, and they pursue that die.

An

An Apology for having loved before.

THey that never had the uſe
Of the Grapes ſurprizing juyce;
To the firſt delicious cup,
All their Reaſon render up:
Neither do nor care to know,
Whether it be the beſt, or no.

So they that are to love inclin'd;
Sway'd by chance, not choice or art:
To the firſt that's fair or kind,
Make a preſent of their heart:
'Tis not ſhe that firſt we love,
But whom dying we approve.

To man that was i'th' evening made,
Stars gave the firſt delight:
Admiring in the glooming ſhade,
Thoſe little drops of light.

Then as *Aurora*, whoſe fair hand
Remov'd him from the skies,
He gazing toward the Eaſt did ſtand,
She entertain'd his eyes.

But when the bright Snn did appear,
All thoſe he gan deſpiſe,
His wonder was determin'd there,
He could no higher riſe.

He neither might, nor wiſht to know
A more refulgent light:

For

For that as mine, your beauties now,
Imploy his utmost sight.

Palamede to Zelinde, Ariana, Lib. 6.

FAirest peice of well-form'd Earth,
Urge not thus your haughty birth :
The power which you have o'er us, lies
Not in your race. but in your eyes.
None but a Prince ! alas, that voice
Confines you to a narrow choice !
Should you no Honey vow to taste,
But what the master Bees have plac't
In compass of their Cells, how small
A portion to your share would fall ?
Nor all appear among those few,
Worthy the stock from whence they grew :
The sap which at the Root is bred
In Trees, through all the Boughs is spred;
But vertues which in Parents shine,
Make not like progress through the Line.
'Tis not from whom, but where we live ;
The place does of those graces give.
Great *Julius* on the Mountains bred,
A flock perhaps, or herd had led.
He that the world subdued, had been
But the best wrastler on the green.
'Tis Art and Knowledge, which draw forth
The hidden Seeds of Native worth :
They blow those sparks, and make them rise
Into such flames as touch the skies.

To

To the old Hero's hence was given
A Pedigree which reach'd to Heaven;
Of mortal Seed they were not held,
Which other mortals ſo excell'd;
And beauty too in ſuch exceſs
As yours, *Zelinde*, claims no leſs.
Smile but on me, and you ſhall ſcorn
Henceforth to be of Princes born.
I can deſcribe the ſhady Grove
Where your lov'd mother ſlept with *Jove*,
And yet excuſe the faultleſs Dame,
Caught with her Spouſes ſhape, and name:
Thy matchleſs form will credit bring,
To all the wonders I ſhall ſing.

FINIS.

Loves Farewell.

TReading the path to Nobler ends,
A long farewell to Love I gave:
Resolv'd my Country and my Friends
All that remain'd of me should have;
And this Resolve no mortall Dame,
None but those eyes could have o'rthrowne.
The Nymph, I dare, nor need not name,
So high, so like her selfe alone:
Thus the tall Oak which now aspires
Above the feares of private fires,
Grown, and design'd for nobler use,
Not to make warm, but build the house;
Though from our meaner flames secure,
Must that which falls from heaven indure.

To Chloris.

CHloris, what's eminent wee know,
Must for some cause be valued so;
Things without use, though they be good,
Are not by us so understood.
The early Rose made to display
Her blushes to the youthfull *May*,
Doth yeeld her sweets, since he is faire,
And courts her with a gentle ayre.
Our stars to shew their excellence,
Not by their light, but influence;
When brighter Comets since still known,
Fatall to all, are lik't by none:
So your admired beauty still
Is by effects made good or ill.

Madam,

AS in some climes the warmer Sun,
Makes it full Summer ere the spring's begun,
And with ripe fruit the bending boughs can load,
Before the Violets dare looke abroad.
So measure not by any common use,
The early love your brighter eyes produce.
When lately your fair hand in womans weed.
Wrapt my glad head, I wish't me so indeed.
That hasty time might never make me grow
Out of those favours you afford me now;
That I might ever such indulgence find,
And you not blush, or thinke your self too kind.
Who now I feare while I these joyes express,
Begin to thinke how you may make them less:
The sound of love makes your soft heart affraide,
And guard it self, though but a child invade,
And innocently at your white breast throw
A dart as white, a Ball of new faln snow.

An Epigram
On a painted Lady with ill teeth.

WEre men so dull they could not see
That *Lyce* painted, should they flee
Like simple Birds into a Net,
So grosly woven and ill set;
Her own teeth would undoe the knot,
And let all goe that she had got.

Those teeth faire *Lyce* must show,
If she would bite: her Lovers, though

Like

Like Birds they stoop at seeming grapes,
Are disabus'd when first she gapes;
The rotten bones discovered there,
Show 'tis a painted Sepulcher.

On a Girdle.

THat which her slender waste confin'd,
Shall now my joyfull temples bind;
No Monarch but would give his C o wne
His Armes might doe what this has done.

It is my Heavens extreamest Spheare,
The pale which held the lovely Deare,
My joy, my griefe, my hope, my Love,
Doe all within this Circle move.

A narrow compas, and yet there
Dwells all that's good, and all that's faire;
Give me but what this Ribban ty'd,
Take all the sun goes round beside.

On Mr. Iohn Fletchers *Playes.*

FLetcher, to thee we doe not only owe,
All these good Playes, but those others too,
Thy wit repeated, does support the Stage,
Credits the last, and entertaines this Age.
No Worthies form'd by any Muse but thine
Could purchase robes, to make themselves so fine;
What brave Commander is not proud to see
Thy brave *Melantius* in his Gallantrie,

Our greatest Ladys love to see their scorne
Out-done by thine, in what themselves have worne,
The Impatient widdow ere the yeare be done,
Sees thy *Aspasia* weeping in her gowne.
  I never yet the Tragick straine assayed.
Deter'd by that inimitable Maide.
And when I venture at the Comicke stile,
Thy scornfull Lady, seemes to mock my toile.
  Thus has thy Muse at once improv'd and marr'd,
Our sport in playes by rendring it too hard.
So when a sort of lusty shepheards throwe,
The barre by turnes, and none the rest out-goe
So farre but that the best are measuring casts,
There emulation, and their pastimes lasts;
But if some braunie Yeoman of the guard
Stepp in and tosse the axeltrie a yard,
Or more beyond the furthest marke, the rest,
Dispairing stand, Their sport is at the best.

To Chloris *upon a favour received.*

CHloris, since first our calme of peace
Was frighted hence, this good we finde.
Your favours with your feares increase,
And growing mischiefs make you kinde.
So the fayre tree which still preserves
Her fruit and state whilst no wind blows,
In stormes from that uprightnesse swerves.
Aud the glad earth about her strowes
With treasure from her yielding boughs.

FINIS.

THE TABLE.

Of the danger his Majesty (being Prince) escaped at the rode at St. Andere. 6

Of His Majesties receiving of the newes of the Duke of Buckinghams *death.* 1

To the King on His Navy. 2

Upon His Majesties repairing of Pauls. 3

To the Queen, *occasioned upon sight of her Majesties Picture.* 11

The apologie of sleep, for not approaching the Lady who can doe any thing but sleepe when she pleaseth. 13

The Country to my Lady of Carlisle. 15

The Countesse of Carlisle *in mourning.* 16

An answer to a Libell against her &c. 17

On my Lady Dorothy Sidneys *Picture.* 18

To Vandike. 19

At Pens-Hurst. 21

At Pens-Hurst. 22

To my Lord of Leicester. 23

To my young Lady Lucy Sidney. 24

Of the Lady who can sleep when shee pleaseth. 25

Of the misreport of her being painted. 26

Of her passing through a crowd of people. 27

A Song, Say lovely dreame. 28

A Song: Behold the brand of beauty tost. 29

To Amoret. 29

The story of Phœbus *and* Daphne *applyed*, &c. 32

Of Mistris Arden. 32

On

The table.

On the discovery of a Ladyes painting. 33
To a Lady from whom he receiv'd a silver pen. 34
On a Brede on divers colours woven by four Ladies. 35
On the head of a Stag, 35
To a Lady in retirement. 36
The Misers Speech in a Maske. 37
To my Lord of Northumberland *upon the death of his Lady.* 38
To my Lord Admirall of his late sicknesse and recovery. 39
On the friendship betwixt Sacharissa *and* Amoret. 41
A la malade 42
Of her Chamber 43
Of loving at first sight. 44
The selfe banished. 45
Of and to the Queene. 46
A Song. Goe lovely Rose. 48
Thirsis. Galatea. 49
Fabula Phœbi & Daphnis. 51
The battell of the summer Islands, in three Cantoes 52
Upon the Death of the Lady Rich. 59
To the Queene Mother upon her landing. 62
A Song. Peace babling Muse. 63
Of Love. 63
To the mutable Faire. 65
Of the taking of Sally. 67
To Mistris Broughton. 68
Puerperium. 70
To Phillis. 71
To Phillis. 72
A Song. While I listen to thy voyce. 73
A Song. Stay Phœbus, *stay.* 73
To Amoret. 74

To

The table.

To my Lord of Falkland. 75
On a Lady who writ in praise of Mira. 76
To one Married to an old Man. 76
For the drinking of Healths. 77
To Flavia *a Song.* 77
Of my Lady Isabella *playing on a Lute.* 78
The Fall. 79
Of Silvia. 80
The Bud. 80
To a Lady singing a Song of his Composing: 81
At the Marriage of the Dwarfs. 82
Upon Ben. Johnson. 83
To Mr. George Sands, *on his Translation of some part of the Bible.* 84
Chloris *and* Hilas. 85
Under a Ladyes Picture. 86
In answer of Sir John Sucklins *Verses.* 86
To A.H. *of the different successe of their Loves.* 89
An Apologie for having Loved before 90
Palamede *to* Zelinde. Ariana, *Lib.6.* 91
Loves Farewell. 93
To Chloris. 93
Madam. As in some climes. 94
An Epigram on a painted Lady with ill teeth 94
On a Girdle. 95
On Mr. John Fletchers *Playes.* 95
To Cloris *upon a Favour received.* 96

FINIS.

Mr. WALLERS Speech in Parliament against the Prelates Innovations.

Mr. Speaker,

VVEE ſhall make it appeare, the errours of Divines who would that a Monarch, can bee abſolute, and that hee can do all things *ad libitum*, receding not onely from their Text, (though that bee wandring too) but from the way their own profeſſion might teach them. *Stare ſuper vias antiquas*, and remove not the ancient bounds and Land-marks, which our Fathers have ſet.

If to bee abſolute, were to bee reſtrained by no Lawes; Then can no King in Chriſtendome bee ſo, for they all ſtand obleidged to the Laws Chriſtian, and we ask no more, for to this Pillar, bee our Priviledges fixt. Our Kings at their *Coronation*, having taken a Sacred Oath, not to infringe them, I am ſorry theſe men take no more care, for the informing of our Faith of theſe things, which they tell us for our Soules health; whileſt wee know them ſo manifeſtly in the wrong way, in that which concernes the Liberties and Priviledges of the Subjects of *England*.

O They

They gain preferment, and then it is no matter; though they neither beleeve themselves, nor are beleeved by others. But since they are so ready, to let loose the Conscience of our Kings, wee are the more carefully to proceed for our protection against this Pulpit-law, by declaring, and reinforcing Municipall Laws of this Kingdom.

It is worthy the observation, how new this opinion, or rather this way of rising, is even amongst themselves.

For, (Mr. *Speaker*) Mr. *Hooker*, who was no refractory man, (as they term it) thinks that the first government was Arbitray, untill it was found, that to live by one mans will, becomes all mens misery; these are his words, and that these were the originall of inventing Laws.

And (Mr. *Speaker*,) if wee looke farther backe, our Histories will tell us, that the Prelates of this Kingdome, have often been the Mediators between the King and his Subjects, to present and pray redresse of their grievances, and had reciprocally then, as much love and reverence from the people.

But these Preachers, more active then their Predecessors, and wiser then the Laws, have fouud out a better form of Goverment.

The King must be a more absolute Monarch, than any of his Pedecessours, and to them he must owe it, though in the mean time, they hazard the hearts of his People, and involve Him into a thousand Difficulties.

For suppose, this forme of Government were inconvenient

venient ; (Mr. Speaker) this is but a Suppoſition ; for this five hundred years it hath not only maintained us in ſafety, but made us victorious over other Nations : But ſuppoſe, this form of Government were inonconvenient ; and they have another *Idea* of one more convenient : We all know, how dangerous Innovations are, though to the better ; and what hazard thoſe Princes run, that enterprize the Change of a long eſtabliſhed Government.

Now (*Mr. Speaker*) of all our Kings that have gone before, and of all that are to ſucceed in this happy race, why ſhould ſo pious, and ſo good a King, be expoſed to this trouble and hazard ? Beſides, that King ſo diverted, can never doe any great matters abroad.

But (*Mr. Speaker*) whileſt theſe men have thus bent their Wits againſt the Law of their Country ; have they not neglected their own profeſſion ? What tares are grown up in the field, which they ſhould have tilled, I leave it to a ſecond conſideration ? not but Religion be the firſt thing in our purpoſes and deſires : But that which is firſt in dignity, is not alwayes to preceed in order of time, for well-being, ſuppoſes a being; and the firſt impediment which men naturally, endeavour to remove, is the want of thoſe things, without which they cannot ſubſiſt. God firſt aſſigned unto *Adam*, maintenance of life, and added to him a title to the reſt of the Creätures, before he appointed a Law to obſerve.

And let me tell you, that if our Adverſaries have any ſuch deſigne, as there is nothing more eaſie, then to impoſe Religion on a people deprived of their Liberties, ſo there is nothing more hard, then to do the ſame upon Free-men.

And therefore (*Mr. Speaker*) I conclude with this motion, that there may be an Order preſently made, that the firſt thing this Houſe goes about, ſhall be the reſtoring of this Nation in generall, to the fundamentall and vitall Liberties, the propriety of our Goods, and freedome of our Perſons: And then We will forthwith conſider of the ſupply deſired.

And thus ſhall We diſcharge the truſt repoſed in us by thoſe that ſent us hither: And His Majeſty ſhall ſee, that we will make more then ordinary haſt to ſatisfie *His demands*; and we ſhall let all thoſe know that ſeek to haſten the matter of ſupply, that they will ſo far delay it, as they give no interruption to the Former.

Mr. WALLERS Speech in Parliament, at a Conference of both Houses in the painted Chamber. 6. *July* 1641.

MY LORDS.

I Am commanded by the House of Commons, to present you with these Articles against Mr. Justice *Crawley*, which when your Lordships shall have been pleased to heare read I shall take leave (according to custome) to say something of what I have collected from the sense of that House concerning the crimes therein conteined.

Here the charge was read conteining his extrajudiciall opinions subscribed, and judgement given for Ship-money, and afterward a declaration in his charge at on assize, that Ship-mony was so inherent a right in the Crown, that it would not be in the power of a Parliament to take it away.

MY LORDS, Not only my wants but my affections render me lesse fit for this imployment: for though it has not been my happinesse to have the Law a part of my breeding, there is no man honours that profession more, or has a greater reverence towards the grave Judges the Oracles thereof. Out of Parliament all our Courts of Justice are governed or directed by them, and when a Parliament is

 call'd

call'd, if your Lordships were not assisted by them, and the House of Commons by other Gentlemen of that Robe, experience tells us it might runne a hazard of being styled *Parliamentum indoctorum*. But as all professions are obnoxious to the malice of the professors, and by them most easily betrayed, so (my Lords) these Articles have told you how these brothers of the Coyfe are become *fratres in malo*; how these sonnes of the Law have torne out the bowells of their mother: But this Judge (whose charge you last heard) in one expression of his excells no lesse his Fellowes, then they have done the worst of their predecessours, in this conspiracy against the Common-wealth. Of the Judgement for Shipmoney, and those extrajudiciall opinions preceding the same (wherein they are joyntly concern'd) you have already heard; how unjust and pernitious a proceeding that was in so publique a Cause, has beene sufficiently expres'd to your Lordships: But this man, adding despaire to our misery, tells us from the Bench, that Ship-money was a Right so inhærent in the Crowne, that it would not be in the power of an Act of Parliament to take it away. Herein (my Lords) he did not onely give as deepe a wound to the Common-wealth as any of the rest, but dipt his dart in such a poyson, that so farre as in him lay it might never receive a cure. As by those abortive opinions subscribing to the subversion of our propriety, before hee heard what could be said for it, he prevented his owne, so by this declaration of his he endevours to prevent the Judgement of your Lordships too, and

and to confine the power of a Parliament, the onely place where this mischiefe might be redrest: Sure he is more wise and learned, then to beleeve himselfe in this opinion, or not to know how ridiculous it would appeare to a Parliament, and how dangerous to himself, and therefore no doubt but by saying no Parliament could abolish this Judgement, his meaning was that this Judgement had abolish't Parliaments.

This imposition of Ship-mony springing from a pretended necessity, was it not enough that it was now grown annuall, but he must intayle it upon the State for ever, at once making necessity inhoerent to the Crowne, and slavery to the Subject? Necessity, which dissolving all Law is so much more prejudiciall to his Majesty then to any of us, by how much the Law has invested his Royall State with a greater power, and ampler fortune, for so undoubted a truth it has ever beene, that Kings as well as Subjects are involv'd in the confusion which necessity produces, that the Heathen, thought their gods also obliged by the same, *Pareamus necessitati quam nec homines nec dii superant*: This Judge then having in his charge at the Assize declar'd the dissolution of the Law by this suppos'd necessity, with what conscience could hee at the same Assize proceed to condeme and punish men, unlesse perhaps hee meant the Law was still in force for our destruction, and not for our preservation, that it should have power to kill, but none to protect us; a thing no lesse horrid then if the Sunne should burne without lighting us, or the earth serve onely to bury and not to feed and nourish us. But (my Lords) to demonstrate that this was a suppositious impos'd necessity, and such as they could remove when they pleas'd, at the last Convention in Parliament a price was set upon it, *for twelve Subsidies you shall reverse this Sentence*; It may be said that so much money would have removed the present necessity, but here was a Rate set upon future necessity. *For twelve Subsidies you shall never suffer necessity again, you shall for ever abolish that judgement*; Here this mystery is revealed, this visour of necessity is pull'd off, and now it appeares that this Parliament of Judges had very frankly and bountifully presented his Majesty with twelve Subsidies to be leavied on your Lordships, and the Commons: Certainly there is no priviledge which more properly belongs to a Parliament, then to open the purse of the Subject, and yet these Judges, who are neither capable of sitting among us in the house of Commons, nor with your Lordships, otherwise then as your assistants, have not only assum'd to themselves this priviledge of Parliament, but presum'd at once to make a present to the Crowne of all that either your Lordships or the Commons of *England* doe, or shall hereafter possesse.

And because this man has had the boldnesse to put the power of Parliament in ballance with the opinion of the Judges, I shall intreat your Lordships to observe by way of comparison the solemne and safe proceeding of the one, with the precipitate dispatch of the other. In Parliament (as your Lordships know well (no new Law can passe, or old be abrogated, till

it

it has been thrice read with your Lordſhips, thrice in the Commons Houſe, and then it receives the Royall Aſſent, ſo that 'tis like gold 7 times purified ; whereas theſe Judges by this one reſolution of thiers, would perſwade his Majeſty, that by naming *neceſſity* he might at once diſſolve (at leaſt ſuſpend) the great Charter 32 times confirm'd by his Royal Progenitours, the petition of Right, and all other Lawes provided for the maintenance of the Right and propriety of the Subject ; a ſtrange force (my Lords) in the ſound of this word *neceſſity*, that like a Charme it ſhould ſilence the Laws, while we are piſpoyl'd of all we have : for that but a part of our goods was taken, is owing to the grace and goodneſſe of the King ; for ſo much as concernes theſe Judges, we have no more left then they perhaps may deſerve to have, when your Lordſhips ſhall have paſſed Judgement upon them : This for the the neglect of their Oaths, and betraying that publique truſt, which for the conſervation of our Lawes was repoſed in them.

Now for the cruelty and unmercifulneſſe of this judgement, you may pleaſe to remember that in the old Law they were forbid to ſeeth a Kid in his mothers milk, of which the received interpretation is, that we ſhould not uſe that to the deſtruction of any creature which was intended for its preſervation ; New (my Lords) God and Nature has given us the Sea as our beſt Guard againſt our Enemies, and our ſhips as our greateſt glory above other Nations, and how barbarouſly would theſe men have let in the ſea upon us, at once to wash away our Liberties, and to overwhelm, if not our Land, all the propriety wee have therein, making the supply of our Navy, a pretence for the ruine of our Nation; for observe I beseech you the fruit and consequence of this judgement, how this money has prosper'd, how contrary an effect it has had to the end for which they pretended to take it: On every County a ship is annually impos'd, and who would not expect, but our seas by this time should be covered with the number of our ships? Alas (my Lords) the daily Complaints of the decay of our Navy tels us how ill ship-money has maintain'd the Soveraignty of the sea: and by the many petitions which we receive from the wives of those miserable Captives at *Algier* (being between 4 and 5 thousand of our Country-men) it does evidently appeare that to make us slaves at home, is not the way to keepe us from being made slaves abroad; so farre has this judgement bin from reliving the present or preventing the future necessity, that as it changed our reall propriety into the shadow of a propriety, so of a feigned it has made a Reall necessity.

A little before the approach of the *Gaules* to *Rome*, while the Romans had yet no apprehension of that danger, there was heard a voyce in the Aire, lowder then ordinary, *The Gaules are come*, which voyce after they had sack'd the Citie, and besieged the Capitoll, was held so ominous, that *Livie* relates it as a Prodigy; This Anticipation of necessity seems to have been no lesse ominous to us; These Judges like ill boading birds

birds have call'd necessity upon the State in a time when I dare say they thought themselves in greatest security; but if it seem superstitious to take this as an Omen, sure I am we may look on it as a cause of the unfained necessity we now suffer, for what regret and discontent had this judgement bred among us? And as when the noyse and tumult in a private house growes so loud, as to be heard into the streets, it calls in the next dwellers either kindly to appease, or to make their own use of the domestick strife; so in all likelyhood our known discontents at home have been a concurrent cause to invite our Neighbours to visite us so much, to the expence and trouble of both these Kingdomes.

And here, my Lords, I cannot but take notice of the most sad effect of this oppression, the ill influence it has had upon the ancient reputation and valour of the English Nation: and no wonder, for if it be true that oppression makes a wise man mad, it may well suspend the courage of the valiant: The same happened to the Romans when for renowne in Armes they most excell'd the rest of the world; the story is but short, 'twas in the time of the *Decem-viri*. (and I think the chief-troublers of our State may make up that number,) The *Decem-viri*, my Lords, had subverted the Lawes, suspended the Courts of Justice; and (which was the greatest grievance both to the Nobility and people) had for some years omitted to assemble the Senate, which was their Parliament; This sayes the Historian did not onely deject the Romans, and make them despaire of their Liberty, but caused them

to

to be lesse valued by their Neighbours : The Sabines take the advantage and invade them ; and now the *Decem-viri* are forc'd to call the long desired Senate , whereof the people were so glad , that *Hostibus belloq; gratiam habuerunt* : This Assembly breaks up in discontent, neverthelesse the warre proceeds; Forces are rais'd, led by some of the *Decem-viri*, and with the Sabines they meet in the Field ; I know your Lordships expect the event ; My Authors words of his Countrey-men are these, *Ne quid ductu aut auspicio Decem-virorum prospere gereretur, vinci se patiebantur,* They chose rather to suffer a present diminution of their Honour, then by victory to confirme the tyranny of their new Masters : At their return from this unfortunate expedition, after some distempers and expostulations of the people, an other Senate, that is a second Parliament, is call'd, and there the *Decem-viri* are questioned, deprived of their Authority, imprisoned, banish'd, and some loose their lives ; and soon after this vindication of their Liberties, the Romans by their better successe made it appeare to the world, that liberty and courage dwell alwayes in the same brest, and are never to be divorced. No doubt, my Lords, but your Justice shall have the like effect upon this dispirited people ; 'tis not the restitution of our ancient Lawes alone, but the restauration of our ancient courage which is expected from yonr Lordships : I need not say any thing to move your just indignation that this man should so cheaply give away that which your noble Ancestors with so much courage and industry

ſtry had ſo long maintain'd: you have often been told how carefull they were, though with the hazard of their lives and fortunes, to derive thoſe Rights and Liberties as entire to poſterity as they received from their Fathers: what they did with labour you may do with eaſe, what they did with danger, you may doe ſecurely, the foundation of our Lawes is not ſhaken with the Engine of Warre, they are onely blaſted with the breath of theſe men,& by your breath may be reſtored.

What Judgements your Predeceſſors have given, and what puniſhments their Predeceſſors have ſuffer'd for offences of this nature, your Lordſhips have already been ſo well informed, that I ſhall not trouble you with a repetition of thoſe precedents: Onely (my Lords) ſomething I ſhall take leave to obſerve of the perſon with whoſe charge I have preſented you, that you may the leſſe doubt of the wilfulneſſe of his offence.

His education in the Inns of Court, his conſtant practice as a Councellour, and his experience as a Judge (conſidered with the miſchiefe he has done) makes it appeare that this Progreſſe of his through the Law, has been like that of a diligent Spie through a Country into which he meant to conduct an enemy.

To let you ſee he did not offend for company, there is one crime ſo peculiar to himſelfe, and of ſuch malignity, that it makes him at once uncapable of your Lordſhips favour, and his own ſubſiſtence incompatible with the right and propriety of the Subject: for if you leave him in a capacity of interpreting the Lawes, has he not already declared his opinion, That your

votes

votes and resolutions against Ship-money are voyd, and that it is not in the power of a Parliament to abolish that Judgement? To him, my Lords, that has thus plaid with the power of Parliament, wee may well apply what was once said to the Goat browsing on the Vine,

Rode, caper, vitem, tamen hinc cum stabis ad aras
In Tua quod fundi cornua possit, erit:

Hee has cropt and infring'd the priviledges of a banish'd Parliament, but now it is returned he may find it has power enough to make a Sacrifice of him, to the better establishment of our Lawes; and in truth what other satisfaction can he make his injur'd Country, then to confirme by his example those Rights and Liberties which he had ruin'd by his opinion?

For the proofes, my Lords, they are so manifest that they will give you little trouble in the disquisition; his crimes are already upon Record, the Delinquent and the Witness is the same; having from severall Seats of Judicature proclaim'd himselfe an Enemy to our Lawes and Nation, *Ex ore suo judicabitur*. To which purpose I am commanded by the Knights, Citizens, and Burgesses of the House of Commons, to desire your Lordships that as speedy a proceeding may bee had against M. Justice *Crawley* as the course of Parliaments will permit.

Master

Mr. WALLERS SPEECH,

In the House of Commons, the fourth of *July*, 1643. being brought to the Bar, and having leave given him by rhe Speaker, to say what he could for himselfe.

Mr. Speaker.

Acknowledge it a great mercy of God, and a great favour from you, that I am once more suffered to behold this Honourable Assembly, I mean not to make use of it to say any thing in my own defence by Justification or denyall of what I have done, I have already confessed enough to make me appeare, worthy not onely to be put out of this House, but out of the World too. All my humble request to you is, that, if I seeme to you as unworthy to live, as I doe to my selfe, I may have the Honour to receive my death from your owne hands, and not bee exposed to a Tryall by the Counsell of Warre: what ever you shall thinke me worthy to suffer in a Parliamentary way, is not like to finde stop any where else.

This (Sir) I hope you will be pleased for your own sakes to grant me, who am already so miserable, that nothing can be added to my calamity, but to be made the occasion of creating a President to your own disadvantage; besides the right I may have to this, consider I beseech you that the eyes of the world are upon

you

you governe in chiefe, and if you should expose your owne members to the punishment of others, it will be thought that you either want Power, or leisure to chastise them your selves; nor let any man despise the ill consequence of such a president as this would be, because hee seeth not presently the inconveniences which may ensue: you have many Armies on Foote, and it is uncerteine how long you may have occasion to use them. Souldiers and Commanders (though I know well they of the Parliaments Army, excell no lesse in modesty then they doe in Courage) are generally of a Nature ready to pretend to the utmost power of this kind, which they conceive to be due to them, and may be too apt upon any occasion of discontent to make use of such a President as this. In this very Parliament you have not bin without some tast of the experience hereof, it is now somewhat more than two yeares since you had an Army in the North, paid and directed by your selves, and yet you may be pleased to remember there was a considerable number of Officers in that Army, which joyned in a Petition or Remonstrance to this House, taking notice of what some of Members had said here, as they supposed to their disadvantage, and did little lesse then require them of you; 'tis true, there had bin some tampering with them, but what has happened at one time, may wisely be thought possible to fall out againe at another.

Sir, I presume but to point you out the danger; if it be not just, I know you will not do me the wrong to expose me to this triall; if it be just your Army may another time require the same justice of you, in their owne behalfe, against some other Member, whom perhaps you would be lesse willing to part with. Necessity has of late forced you into untrodden paths ; and in such a case as this where you have no president of your own, you may not doe amisse to looke abroad upon other States and Senates, which exercise the Supreame Power, as you now doe here.

I dare confidently say you shall finde none either Antient or Moderne, which ever exposed any of their owne order to be tryed for his life by the Officers of their Armies abroad, for what he did, while he resided among them in the Senate.

Among the Romans the practice was so contrary, that some inferiour Officers in their Army farre from the City, having been sentenced by their Generall or Commander in chief, as deserving death by their Discipline of Warre, have neverthelesse (because they were Senators) appealed thither, and the cause has received a new hearing in the Senate. Not to use more words to perswade you to take heed that you wound not your selves thorough my sides in violating the Priviledges belonging to your own persons, I shall humbly desire you to consider likewise the nature of my offence, (not but that I should be much ashamed to say any thing in diminution therof; God knowes 'tis horrid enough for the evill it might have occasioned) but if you looke neare it, it may perhaps appeare to be rather a Civill then a Martiall crime and so to have

Title to a Triall at the common law of the land; ther may justly be some difference put between mee and others in this businesse.

I have had nothing to do with the other Army, or any intention to begin the offer of violence to any body, It was only a civill pretence to that which I then foolishly conceived to be the right of the subject. I humbly refer it to your considerations, and to your consciences. I know you will take care not to to shed the blood of War in Peace that blood by the law of War, which hath a right to betryed by the Law of Peace.

For so much as concerns my selfe and my part in this businesse, (if I were worthy to have any thing spoken or patiently heard in my behalfe) this might truly be said, that I made not this business, but found it, 'twas in other mens hands long before it was brought to me, and when it came I extended it not, but restrained it. For the Propositions of letting in part of the Kings Army, or offering violence to the Members of this House, I ever disallowed and utterly rejected them.

What it was that moved me to entertain discourse of this businesse, so far as I did, I will tell you ingeniously, and that rather as a warning for others, than that it make any thing for my selfe; it was only an impatience of the inconveniences of the present War, looking on things with a carnall eye, and not minding that which chiefly (if not onely) ought to have been considered, the inestimable value of the Cause you have in hand, the Cause of God and of Religion, and the necessities you are forced upon for the maintenance of the same;

ſame ; as a juſt puniſhment for this neglect, it pleaſed God to deſert and ſuffer me with a fatall blindneſſe, to be led on,and ingaged in ſuch Counſels as were wholly diſproportioned to the reſt of my life ; This (Sir) my own Conſcience tells me was the cauſe of my failing, and not malice, or any ill habit of minde,or diſpoſition toward the Common-wealth, or to the Parliament: for from whence ſhould I have it? If you look on my Birth, you will not find it in my blood: I am of a ſtock which hath born you better fruit,if you look on my education, it hath been almoſt from my child-hood in this Houſe, and among the beſt ſort of men; and for the whole practice of my life till this time, if another were to ſpeake for me,he might reaſonably ſay,that neither my actions out of Parliament, nor my expreſſions in it, have ſavoured of diſaffection or malice to the Liberties of the People, or Priviledges of Parliament.

Thus Sir, I have ſet before your eyes,both my perſon and my caſe, wherein I ſhall make no ſuch defence by denying, or extenuating any thing I have done, as ordinarily Delinquents doe, my addreſſe to you, and all my Plea ſhall onely be ſuch as Children uſe to their Parents, I have offended ; I confeſſe it, I never did any thing like it before ; it is a paſſage unſuitable to the whole courſe of my life beſide,and for the time to come, as God that can bring light out of darkneſſe, hath made this buſineſſe in the event uſefull to you, ſo alſo hath he to me: you have by it made an happy diſcovery of your Enemies,and I of my ſelfe,and the evil principles I walkt by ; ſo that if you look either on what I

 have

have been heretofore, or what I now am, and by Gods grace assisting me, shall alwayes continue to be, you may perhaps thinke me fit to be an example of your compassion and clemency.

Sir, I shal no sooner leave you, but my life wil depend on your breath, & not that alone, but the subsistence of some that are more innocent. I might therefore shew you my Children, whom the rigour of your Justice would make compleat Orphanes, being already Motherless. I might shew you a Family, wherein there are some unworthy to have their share in that mark of Infamy which now threatens us: But something there is, which if I could shew you, would move you more then all this, it is my Heart, which abhors what I have done more, & is more severe to it selfe, then the severest Judge can be. A heart (Mr. Speaker) so awakened by this affliction, and so intirely devoted to the Cause you maintain, that I earnestly desire of God to incline you, so to dispose of me, whether for life or death, as may most conduce to the advancement therof.

Sir, not to trouble you any longer, if I dye, I shall dye praying for you; if I live, I shall live serving you, and render you back the use and imployment of all those dayes yon shall adde to my life.

After this having withdrawn himselfe, he was called in again, and (being by the Speaker required thereto) gave them an exact account how he came first to the knowledge of this businesse; as also what Lords were acquainted therwith, or had engaged themselves therein.

FINIS.

Courteous Reader, these Books following are printed for *Humphrey Moseley*, at the *Princes Armes* in St. *Pauls* Church-yard.

Various Histories, with curious Discourses in humane Learning, &c.

1 HIstoricall relations of the united Provinces of *Flanders*, by Cardinall *Bentivoglio*: Englished by the Right Honorable *Henry* Earle of *Monmouth*. Fol.

2. The History of the Warrs of *Flanders*, written in *Italian* by that learned and famous Cardinal *Bentivoglio*; Englished by the Right Honorable *Henry* E. of *Monmouth*. The whole worke Illustrated with a Map of the 17. Provinces, and above 20 Figures of the chiefe Personages mentioned in this History. Fol.

3. The History of the Warrs of the Emperor *Justinian*, with the *Persians*, *Goths*, and *Vandalls*, written in Greek by *Procopius* of *Cæsaria* in eight Bookes, translated into English by Sir *Henry Holcroft*. Knight. Fol.

4. *De Bello Belgico*, the History of the Low-Country Warrs, written in Latine by *Famianus Strada*, in English by Sir *Robert Stapylton*, Illustrated with divers Figures. Fol.

5. The use of passions, written by *I. F.* Senalt, and put into English by *Henry*, Earle of *Monmouth* 8°.

6. Judicious and Select Essaies and observations by the Renowned and learned Knight, Sir *Walter Raleigh*, with his Apology for his Voyage to *Guiana*. Fol.

7. The Compleat Horsman and Expert Farrier in two books, by *Thomas De Grey* Esquire, newly printed with additions. in 4° *1656*.

8. Unheard-of curiosities concerning the Talismanicall Sculpture of the *Persians*. The *Horoscope* of the Patriarchs, and the judgment of the Starrs, by *J. Gaffarel*, Englished by *Edmund Chilmead, Ch. Ch. Oxon*.

9. The History of the *Inquisition*, composed by *R. F. Servita*, the compiler of the History of the Coun-

cill of Trent, in 8°. translated out of Italian.

10. *Biathanatos*, a Paradox of self-murther, by Dr. *Jo. Donne*, Dean of St. *Pauls* London.

11. The Gentlemans Exercise, or the Art of limning, painting, and blazoning of Coats and Armes, *&c.* by *Henry Peacham* Master of Arts, 4°.

12. M. *Howels* History of *Lewis* the thirteenth King of *France*, with the life of his Cardinal *de Richelieu*. Fol.

13. Mr. *Howels Epistolæ Ho-elianæ.* Familiar letters Domestick and Forren, in six Sections partly Historicall, Politicall, Philosophicall, the first Volume with Additions. 8°.

14. Mr. *Howels* new volume of Familiar letters partly Historicall, Politicall, Philosophicall, the second Volume with many Additions. 8o.

15. Mr. *Howels* third Volume of Additionall letters of a fresher date, never before published. 8°.

16. Mr. *Howels Dodono's Grove,* or the *Vocall Forest*, the first part, in 12°. with many Additions.

17. Mr. *Howels Dodona's Grove*, or the *Vocall Forest*, the second part, in 8°, never printed before.

18. Mr. *Howels, Englands Teares* for the present wars.

19. Mr. *Howels Pre-eminence* and Pedegree of Parliament, in 12°.

20. Mr. *Howels* Instructions and Directions for Forren Travels, in 12° with divers Additions for Travelling into Turky, and the Levant parts.

21. Mr. *Howels* Vote, or a Poem Royall presented to his late Majesty, in 4°.

22. Mr. Howels *Angliæ Suspiria & lachrymæ, in* 12°.

23. *Marques Virgilio Malvezzi's Romulus* and *Tarquin*, Englished by Hen. Earl of *Monmouth*, in 12°.

24. *Marques Virgilio Malvezzi's David* persecuted, Englished by *Ro. Ashly*. Gent. in 12°.

25. *Marques Virgilio Malvezzi*, of the successe and chiefe events of the Monarchy of Spain, in the year 1639.

1639. of the revolt of the Catalonians from the King of Spain. Englished by *Rob. Gentilis* Gent. in. 12°.

26. *Marques Virgilio Malvezzi's* considerations on the lives of *Alcibiades*, and *Coriolanus*, Two famous Roman Commanders, Englished by *Rob. Gentilis.*

27. *Policy unveiled*, or *Maximes of State*, done into English by the Translator of *Gusman*, in 4°.

28. Gracious priveleges granted by the King of Spaine to our English Merchants, in 4°.

29. Englands looking in and out by Sr. *Ralph Maddison*, Knight, 4°.

30. *Gratiæ Ludentes*, jests from the University.

31. The Antipathy between the *French* and the *Spanyard*, an ingenious translation out of Spanish.

32. Mr. *Birds* grounds of Grammar, in 8°.

33. Mr. *Bulwers* Phylocophus, or the Deafe and Dumb mans friend, in 12°.

34. Mr. *Bulwers* Pathomyotomia, or a Deflection of the significative Muscles of the Affections of the Mind, 12°.

35. An Itinenary containing a voyage made through Italy in the yeares 1646, 1647. illustrated with divers Figures of Antiquity, never before published, by *John Raymond*, Gent. in 120.

Books in Humanity lately Printed.

36. THe History of Life and Death, or the prolongation of Life, written by *Francis* Lord *Verulam*, Viscount St. *Alban* in 12°.

37. The naturall and experimentall History of Winds, written in Latine by *Francis* Lord *Verulam* Viscount St. *Alban*, translated into English by an admirer of the learned Author. 12°.

38. The life of the most learned Father *Paul*, Authour of the History of the Councill of *Trent*, translated out of *Italian* by a person of quality. 8°.

39. Paradoxes, Problems, Characters, & . by Dr. *Donn* Dean of St *Paul's*, to which is added a booke of Epigrams, written in Latin by the same Author, translated by *Iasper Main*. D. D. 12°.

40. *Ignatius* his conclave, a Satyr written by Dr. *Donne* Deane of St. *Paul's*. 12°.

41. A Discovery of subterraneall Treasure, *viz*. of all manner of Mines and Minerals, from the Gold, to the Coale, with plain directions and rules for the finding of them in all Kingdomes, and Countries, written by *Gabriel* Platt. 4°.

42. *Richardi Gardiner, ex Æde Christi Oxon. specimen Oratorium*. 8°.

43. The Soveraignty of the British Seas, written by that learned Knight Sir *Iohn Burroughes* Keeper of the Records in the Tower. 12°.

44. *Grammatica Burlesa*, or a new English Grammar made plaine and easie for Teacher and Schollar, composed by *Edward Burles* Master of Arts.

45. Artificiall Arithmetick containing the Quintessence of the Golden Rule, the true valuation of all Annuities, also to find the distance at one station ; An Art never till now published, usefull for Merchants, Gunners, Seamen, and Surveyors, by *Robert Iager* of *Sandwich* in *Kent* Gent.

46. Naturall and Divine Contemplations of the Passions and Faculties of the Soul of Man in three books, written by *Nicholas Moseley* Esq. 8°.

Severall Sermons, with other exeellent Tracts in Divinity, written by some most eminent and learned Bishops, and Orthodox Divines.

47. A *Manuall* of private Devotions & Meditations for every day in the week, by the right reverend Father in God, *Lancelot Andrews* late Lord Bishop of *Winchester*, in 24°.

48. A

48. A *Manuall* of Directions for the Sick, with many sweet Meditations and Devotions, by the right reverend Father in God, *Lancelot Andrews*, late Lord Bishop of *Winchester*, in 24°.

49. Ten Sermons upon severall occasions, preached at St. *Pauls* Crosse, and elsewhere, by the Right reverend Father in God, *Arthur Lake*, late Lord Bishop of Bath and Wells. in 4°.

50. Six Sermons upon severall occasions, preached at Court before the Kings Majesty, and elsewhere, by that late learned and reverend Divine, *John Donne*, Dr. in Divinity, and Dean of St. *Pauls London*, in 4°.

51. Private Devotions in six Letanies, with directions and Prayers for the dayes of the weeke and Sacrament, for the houre of Death, and the day of judgment, and two daily prayers, for the Morning and Evening, written by Dr. *Henry Valentine*, 24°.

52. A Key to the Key of Scripture, or an exposition with notes upon the Epistle to the Romans, the three first chapters, by *William Sclater*, Dr. in Divinity and Minister of the word of God at *Pitmister* in *Somersetshire*, in 4°.

53. *Sarah* and *Hagar*, or the sixteenth Chapter of Genesis opened in ninteen Sermons, being the first legitimate Essay of the pious labours of that learned, Orthodox, and indefatigable Preacher of the Gospell, Mr. *Josias Shute*. B. D. and above 33 years Rector of St *Mary Woolnoth* in *Lombardstreet*, in Folio.

54. Christ's Tears with his love & affection towards Jerusalem, delivered in sundry Sermons upon *Luke* 19. *v*. 41, 42. by *Richard Maden*, B.D. late of *Magdalen Colledge in Cam*. in .4°.

55, Three Sermons *viz*. The benefit of contentation, The Affinity of the faithfull, and The lost sheep found, by Mr. Henry *Smith*. 4°.

56. Ten Sermons preached upon severall *Sundayes*, and

and Saints dayes, by *Peter Hauſted* Mr. in Arts, and Curat at *Uppingham* in *Rutland*, in 4°.

57. Eighteen Sermons preached upon the Incarnation and Nativity of our bleſſed Lord and Saviour Jeſus Chriſt, wherein the greateſt miſteries of Godlineſs are unfolded, to the capacity of the Weakeſt Chriſtian, by *Iohn Dawſon Oxon.* in 4°.

58. The Hiſtory of the Defenders of the Faith, diſcourſing the ſtate of Religion in England during the Reigns of King *Henry* 8. *Edward* 6. Queen *Mary*, and Queen *Elizabeth.* by *C. L.* in 4°.

59. Chriſtian Divinity, written by *Edmund Reeve* Batchelour in divinity, in 4°.

60. The Communion-Book Catechiſm expounded by *Edmund Reeve* Batchelour in Divinity, in 4°.

61. The true and abſolute Biſhop, wherein is ſhewed how Chriſt is our onely ſhepheard and Biſhop of our ſoules, by *Nicolas Darton*, Maſter in Arts, in 4°.

62. A deſcription of the New-born Chriſtian, or a lively pattern of the Saint militant child of God, written by *Nicholas Hunt*, Maſter in Arts, in 4°.

63. Divine Meditations upon the 91. Pſalm, and on the Hiſtory of *Agag* King of *Amalek*, with an Eſſay of Friendſhip written by an honourable perſon,

64. An Hiſtoricall Anatomy of Chriſtian Melancholy, by *Edmund Gregory Oxon*, in 8°.

65. *Lazarus* his Reſt, a Sermon preached at the Funerall of that pious, learned, and Orthodox Divine, Mr. *Ephrim Udall*, by *Thomas*, *Reeve*, B. D :

66. The Survey of Man, in a Sermon as it was delivered by Mr. *John Biſhop* at his Fathers funerall.

67. *Enchiridion* containing inſtitutions Divine and Morall, written by *Francis Quarles*, 24°.

Books in Divinity Lately Printed.

68. THE Pſalmes of *David* from the new Tranſlation of the Bible, turned into Meter, to be

ſung

sung after the old tunes used in the Churches; by the Right Reverend Father in God *Henry King* Bishop of *Chichester*.12°.

69. Choice Musick for three voices, and a thorough-Base composed by Mr. *Henry* and Mr. *William Lawes*, brothers and servants to his late Majesty; with divers Elegies set in Musick by severall friends upon the death of Mr. *William Lawes*.4°.

70. Letters between the Lord *George Digby* and Sir *Kenelm Digby* Knight, concerning Religion. 8°.

71. Essaies in Divinity by Dr. *Donn. D.* of Saint *Paul's*, before he entred into holy orders. 12°.

72. Publike devotions, or a Collection of Prayers used at sundry times by divers Reverend and godly Divines, together with divine implorations, and an introduction to prayer.24°.

73. The Sinners Tears in Meditations and Prayers by *Thomas Fettiplace* of Peterhouse *Camb.* 12°.

74. *Quæstio Quodlibetica*, or a discourse whether it be lawfull to take use for mony by R. F. Knight.

75. *Sions* Prospect in its first view presented in a summary of Divine Truths consenting with the faith professed by the Church of *England*, confirmed from Scripture and reason, composed by *Mr. Robert Mossom* Minister:4°.

76. *Flores Solitudinis*, certaine rare and elegant pieces, *viz*. Two excellent discourses. 1 Of Temperance and Patience. 2 Of life and death by *I. E. Nieremrbergius*. The World contemned; by *Eucherius*, Bishop of *Lions*. And the life of *Paulinus* Bishop of *Nola*, collected in his sicknesse and retirement, by *Henry Vaughan*.

77. 14. Sermons on severall Texts of Scripture with a Catechism written by *Willam Gay* Rector of *Buckland*.

Choyce Poems with excellent Translations, by the most eminent wits of this age.

78. Epigrammata *Thomæ Mori Angli*, in 16°.

79. *Fragmenta Aurea*, a collection of all the incom-

Parable Pieces written by Sr. *Iohn Sucklin* Knight, 8°.

80. Poems, Songs, Sonnets, Elegies, and Letters by *Iohn Donne*, with Elegies on the Authors death, to which is added divers Copies under his own hand, never before in print. 8°.

81. Juvenalls 16. Satyrs tranflated by Sir *Robert Stapylton*, wherein is contained a Survey of the manners and actions of Mankind, with Annotations, 8°.

82. *Mufæus* on the loves of *Hero* and *Leander*, with *Leander's* letter to *Hero*, and her anfwer, taken out of *Ovid*, with Annotations by Sir *Robert Staplyton*, in 12°.

83. Poems, &c. written by Mr. *Edward Waller* of *Beconsfield*, Efq. 8°.

84. *Paftor Fido*, the faithfull Shepheard, a Paftorall, newly tranflated out of the Originall, by Mr. *Richard Fanfhaw*, Efq; 4°.

85. Poems, with a difcovery of the Civill Warrs of Rome, by Mr. *Richard Fanfhaw*, Efq; in 4°.

86. *Europa*, *Cupid* crucified, *Venus* Vigils, with Annotations, by *Thomas Stanley*, Efq; 8°.

87. Coopers Hill, a Poem written by Mr, *John Denham* Efq, the 2d Edition with Additions, 4°.

88. *Medea*, a Tragedy written in Latin by *Lucius Annæus Seneca*, Englifhed by Mr. *Edward Sherburn* Efq; with Annotations, 8°.

89. *Seneca's* anfwer to *Lucilius* his Quære, why good men fuffer misfortunes, feeing there is a Divine providence, Englifhed by Mr. *Edward Sherburn*, Efq; 8°.

90. *Madagafcar* with other Poems, by Sr. *W. Davenant*.

91. Poems with a Mafque by *Thomas Carew* Efq;. Gentleman of the Privie Chamber to his late Majeftie, revived and enlarged with Aditions, 8°.

92. Poems of Mr. *John Milton*, with a Mafque prefented at *Ludlow* Caftle before the Earle of *Bridgewater*, then Prefident of *Wales*, 8°.

93. Poems, &c. with a Mafque called The Triumph of

of Beauty, by *James Shirley*, Gent. 8°.

94. The Miſtriſs, or ſeverall Copies of love-verſes, written by Mr. *Abraham Cowley*. 8o.

95. Stepps to the Temple, ſacred Poems with the delights of the Muſes upon ſeverall occaſions by *Richard Craſhaw* of *Cambridge*. 12°.

96. Divine Poems written by *Francis Quarles* 8°.

97. *Claraſtella*, with other occaſionall Poems, Elegies, Epigrams, Satyrs, written by *R. Heath*. Eſq:

98. Poems written by Mr. *William Shakſpeare*.

99. *Arnalte & Lucenda*, or the melancholy Knight, a Poem tranſlated by L. *Laurence*. 4°.

100. The Odes of *Caſimire*, tranſlated, by Mr. *George Hills* of *Newark*. 12°.

101. Alarum to Poets by *I*. L. 4°.

102. *Fragmenta Poetica* or Miſcellanies of Poeticall Muſings, by *Nich. Murford* Gent. 12°.

103. *Hymnus Tabaci, Authore Raphaele Thorio*. 8°.

104. *Hymnus Tabaci*, a Poem in Honour of Tobacco Heroically compoſed by *Raphael Thorius*, made Engliſh by *Peter Hauſted* Mr. of Arts, *Camb*. 8°.

105. *Olor Iſcanus*, a Collection of ſome ſelect Poems, and Tranſlations, written by Mr. *Henry Vaughan*

106. *Argalus and Parthenia* by *Francis Quarles*.

107. The Academy of Complements wherein Ladies, Gentlewomen, Schollers and ſtrangers may accommodate their Courtly practiſe with gentile Ceremonies, complementall, amorous, high expreſſions and forms of ſpeaking, or writing of Letters, moſt in faſhion, with Additions of many witty Poems and pleaſant New ſongs. 12°.

Poems lately Printed.

107. POems and Tranſlations, the compleat works of *Thomas Stanley* Eſq; 8°.

105. Choice Poems with Comedies and Tragedies,

dies,by Mr. *William Cartwright* late ftudent of Ch. Ch. in *Oxford*, and Proctor of the Univerfity. The Aires and fongs fet by Mr. *Henry Lawes*, fervant to his late Majefty in his publick and private Mufick.

108. Herodian of *Alexandria*, his Imperiall Hiftory of twenty Roman *Cæfars*, and Emperours of his time, firft written in Greek,and now converted into an Heroick Poem by *C. Stapleton.* 4°.

109. The Card of Courtfhip or the Language of love fitted to the humours of all degrees, fexes and Conditions.

Incomparable Comedies and Tragedies written by feveral Ingenious Authors.

110. Comedies and Tragedies written by *Francis Beaumont*, and *John Fletcher*, never printed before, and now publifhed bythe Authors Originals Copies,contayning 34 playes,and a Mafque, Fol.

111. The Elder Brother
112. The Scornfull Lady
113. The Woman Hater
114. *Thierry* and *Theodoret*
115. *Cupids* Revenge
116. Monfieur *Thomas*
117. The two Noble kinfmen
} by *Francis Beaumont.* and *Iohn Fletcher.*

118. The Country Captain and the Variety, two Comedies written by a perfon of Honour. 12°.

119. The Sophy,a Tragedy writen by Mr.*Iohn Denham* Efq,Fol.

120. *Brennoralt*,or the difcontented Collonel,a Tragedy written by Sir *Iohn Suckling* Knight.4°.

121. The deferving Favorite by Mr. Lod.*Carlel.*

122. *Albovine* King of Lombardy
123. The Juft Italian
124. The Cruel Brother
125. The Unfortunate Lovers
126. Love and Honour
} by *Sir William Davenant.*

127. The Sophiſter by Dr. Z.
128. Revenge of *Buſſy D Ambois* } *George Chapman*
129. *Byrons* Conſpiracy
130. *Byrons* Tragedy.
131. Contention for Honour and riches } *J. Shirley*
132. Triumph of Peace in 4°.
133. The Dutcheſs of Malfy by *John Webſter.*
134. The Northern laſs by *Richard Broome.*

135. The Cid, a Tragicomedy tranſlated out of French by *Joseph Rutter* Gent. 12°.

136. The Wild Gooſe Chaſe a Comedy written by Fr. *Beaumont* and *John Fletcher.* Fol.

137. The Widow, a Comedy by *Ben: Johnſon, John Fletcher,* and *T: Middleton.*

138. The Changling by *T Middleton* and *Rowley.* 4°.

239. Six new plaies. 1. The Brothers. 2. The Siſters. 3. The Doubtfull Heir. 4. The Impoſture. 5. The Cardinall. 6. The Court-Secret, by *I. Shirley.*

140. Five new plaies. 1. A mad couple well matcht. 2 The Novella. 3. The Court Begger. 4. The City Wit. 5. The Damoiſelle, by *Richard Broome*

141. The Tragedy of *Alphonſus* Emperor of *Germany*, by *George Chapman* 4°.

142. Two Tragedies. *viz.* *Cleopatra* Queen of *Ægypt*, and *Agrippina* Empreſſe of *Rome*, by *Thomas May* Eſq.

Playes lately Printed.

143. THe Gentleman of *Venice*, A Tragi-Comedy by *James Shirley.*

144. The Polititian, a Tragedy by *James Shirley.*

145. The Paſſionate Lovers in two parts, by Mr. *Lodowick Carlel.*

146. *Mirza*, A Tragedy, really acted in *Perſia* with Annotations by *Robert Barron* Eſq;.

147. Three new playes, *viz.* 1 The Baſhfull Lover. 2 The Guardian. 3 The very woman, by *Phillip Maſſenger,* Gent.

New

New and Excellent Romances.

148. CAſſandra the Fam'd Romance, the whole work in five parts, written in French, and now Elegantly rendered into Engliſh by a perſon of quality, Fol.

149. *Ibrahim* or the Illuſtrious *Baſſa*, an excellent new Romance, the whole worke in foure parts, written in French by *Monſieur de Scudery*, and now Engliſhed by *Henry Cogan* Gent. Fol.

150. *Artamenes*, or the Grand *Cyrus*, an excellent new Romance, written by that famous wit of France, *Monſieur de Scudery* Governour of *Noſtre-dame*, and now Engliſhed by *F. G.* Eſq;. Fol.

151. The continuation of *Artamenes*, or the Grand *Cyrus*, that excellent new Romance, being the third and fourth parts, written by that Famous wit of *France*, *Monſieur de Scudery* Governour of *Noſtre-dame*, and now Engliſhed by *F. G.* Eſq;. Fol.

152. The third Volume of *Artamenes* or the Grand *Cyrus*, that excellent new Romance, being the fift and fixt parts, written by that famous wit of *France*, *Monſieur de Scudery* Governour of *Noſtre-dame*, and now Engliſhed by *F. G.* Eſq;. Fol.

153. The fourth Volume of *Artamenes*, or the Grand *Cyrus*, that Excellent new Romance, being the ſeaventh and eighth parts, written by that famous Wit of *France*, *Monſieur de Scudery* Governour of *Noſtre-dame*, and now engliſhed by *F. G.* Eſq;. Fol.

154. The Hiſtory of *Polexander*, a Romance, Engliſhed by *William Browne* Gent. Fol.

155. The Hiſtory of the Baniſhed Virgin, a Romance tranſlated by I. H. Eſq;. Fol.

156. *Caſandra* the fam'd Romance, the three firſt books, Elegantly rendred into Engliſh by the Right Honorable the Lord *George Digby*. 8°.

157. The Hiſtory of *Philoxipes* and *Policrite*, a Romance

mance, made Engliſh by an honorable perſon. 8°.

158. The Hiſtory of *Don Feniſe*, a new Romance, written in Spaniſh by *Franciſco de las Coveras*, Engliſhed by a Perſon of Honour. 8°.

159. *Aurora Iſmenia*, and the Prince, with *Oronta* the Cyprian Virgin, tranſlated by *Thomas Stanley* Eſq;.

160. *Cleopatra*, a new Romance, Engliſhed by a Gent. of the Inner Temple, in 8°.

161. *La Stratonica* or the unfortunate Qeene, a new Romance, tranſlated into Engliſh.

162. Choice Novels, and Amorous Tales written by the moſt refined wits of *Italy*, newly tranſlated into Engliſh by a perſon of quality. in 8°.

163. *Niſſena*, a new Romance, Engliſhed by an Honorable perſon, in 8°.

164. *Dianea*, a new Romance, written in Italian by *Gio Franciſco Loredano*, a Noble Venetian, Engliſhed by Sir *Aſton Cockaine*, in 8°.

Bookes lately printed for Humphrey Moſeley.

165. A German Diet, or the Ballance of *Europe*, wherein the power and weakneſſe, glory, and reproach, Vertues and Vices, Plenty and Wants, Advantages and Defects, Antiquity and Modernes of all the Kingdomes and ſtates of Chriſtendome are Impartially poiz'd by *James Howel* Eſq;. Fol.

166. *Renatus des Cartes'*, excellent compendium of Muſick with neceſſary and juditious Animadverſions thereupon, by a perſon of Honour, Illuſtrated with divers figures in 4°.

167. The Scarlet Gowne, or the Hiſtory of the lives of all the preſent Cardinals of *Rome*, written in Italian and Engliſhed by *Henry Cogan*, Gent. 8°.

168. A diſcourſe of conſtancy, by *Juſtus Lipſius*, faithfully Engliſhed by R. G. ſometimes of *Ch. Ch. Oxon.* containing many ſweet conſolations for all that

are

are afflicted in body, or in mind. 12°.

169. *Le Chemin abrege*, or a compendious Method for the attaining of Sciences in a ſhort time, with the Statutes of the Academy of Cardinall *Richelieu*, Engliſhed by R. G. Gent.

170. The Academy of Eloquence, containing a compleat Engliſh Rhethorick, with common places and formes to ſpeake and write fluently according to the preſent mode, together with letters amorous and morall, by *Thomas Blunt*. Gent. 12°.

171. The Secretary in faſhion, or a compendious and refined way of expreſſion in all manner of letters, with inſtructions how to write letters of all ſorts, compoſed in French by *P.* Sr *de la Serre*, in 8°.

172. *Curia Politiæ*, or the Apologies of ſeverall Princes juſtifying to the World their moſt eminent actions by the ſtrength of Reaſon, and the moſt exact rules of Policy, by the acurate pen of *Monſieur de Scudery*, Governer of *Noſtre-dame*, and now Engliſhed with the figures of many Emperors and Kings.

173. *Ζωοτομία*, or obſervations on the preſent manners of the Engliſh, briefly anatomizing the living by the dead, with an uſefull detection of the Mountebanks of both ſexes by *Richard Whitlock* M.D. late fellow of all Souls Colledge in *Oxon* 8°. 174

174. *Scholæ Wintonienſis Phraſes Latinæ* The Latine Phraſes of *Winchester* School, corrected and much augmented with Poeticalls added, and four Tracts. 1. Of words not to be uſed by elegant Latiniſts. 2. The difference of words like one another in ſound or ſignification. 3. Some words governing a ſubjunctive mood not mentioned in Lillies Grammer. 4. Concerning χρεία & γνώμη for entring children upon making of Themes, by H. *Robinſon* D. D. ſometimes ſchool-maſter of *Wincheſter* Colledge, publiſhed for the common uſe and benefit of Grammer ſchools.

175. *A-*

175. *Atheifmus Vapulans*, or a Treatife againft Atheifm rationally confuting the Atheifts of thefe times by *William Towers*, late ftudent of Ch. Ch. *Oxon.*

176. *De Juramenti Obligatione promiffori Prælectiones Septem.* Of the Obligation of Promiffory Oathes, feven Lectures read in the Divinity Schools at *Oxford* by *Robert Sanderfon D. D.* and englifhed by his late Majefties appointment. 8°.

177. Politick Maxims and obfervations written by the moft learned *Hugo Grotius*, tranflated for the eafe and benefit of the Englifh ftatefmen by H. C. S. T. B.

178. The perfect Horfeman or the experienc'd fecrets of Mr. *Markhams* fifty yeares practice, fhewing how a man may come to be a Generall Horfe--man by the knowledge of thefe feven Offices, *Viz.* The { Breeder, Feeder } { Ambler, Rider } { Keeper, Buyer } Farrier. *Publifhed with fome Additions by* Lancelot Thetford *Practitioner in the fame Art.* 40. *yeares.*

179. Divine Poems written by *Tho. Wafhborn.* B. D.

180. *Buxtorf's* Epitome of his Hebrew Grammar, Englifhed by *John Davis* Mr. of Arts.

181. *Fafciculus Poematum & Epigrammatûm Mifcelaneorum Authore Iohanne Donne.* D.D.

182. *Poemata Græca & Latina, à Gulielmo Cartwright,* C. C. *Oxon.*

183. The Marrow of Complements, containing Amorous Epiftles, complementall entertainments, Dialogues, fongs, and Sonnets, prefentations of gifts, inftructions for Woers, with other pleafant paffages.

Bookes newly Printed for Humphrey Mofeley.

184 THe fifth Volume of *Artamenes*, or the *Grand Cyrus*, that excellent new Romance; being the ninth and tenth Parts: Written by that famous wit of *France, Monfieur de Scudery,* Governour of *Noftre-dame*

dame, and now engliſhed by *F. G.* Eſq.

185 *Eliſe*, or, Innocency guilty; a new Romance, tranſlated into Engliſh by *John Jennings* Gent.

186 *Clelia*, an excellent new Romance, written in French, by the exquiſite pen of *Monſieur de Scudery*, Governour of *Noſtredame de la Gard.*

187 *Coralbo*, a new Romance in three Bookes; written in Italian by *Cavalier Gio Franceſco Biondi*, and now faithfully rendred into Engliſh.

188 The *Luſiad*, or, *Portugalls* Hiſtoricall Poem; tranſlated into Engliſh by *Richard Fanſhaw*, Eſq.

189 The Hiſtory of *Philoſophy*, the firſt Part; by *Tho. Stanley*, Eſq.

190 The Hiſtory of the Kingdome of *Naples*, with the lives of all their Kings; written by that famous Antiquary, *Scipio Mazzella*, with an Addition of what happened during the Rebellion of *Maſſaniello*, and continued to this preſent yeare, by *I. H.* Eſq;.

191 Mr. *Howel*'s fourth Volume of familiar *Letters*, never publiſhed before.

192 *Manziny*, his moſt exquiſite Academicall Diſcourſes upon ſeverall choice Subjects; turned into French by that famous Wit, *Monſieur de Scudery*, and into Engliſh by an Honourable Lady.

193 The *Engliſh Treaſury of Wit and Language*, digeſted into common places, by *Iohn Cotgrave*, Gent.

194 *Luſus Serius*, a Philoſophicall Diſcourſe, of the ſuperiority of the Creatures, by *Michael Mayerus*.

195 The *Aphoriſms* of *Hippocrates*, with a ſhort Comment on them; taken out of *Galen*, *Heurnius*, *Fuchſius*, &c.

196 *Euphrates*, or, the waters of the Eaſt, by *Eugenius Philalethes*.

197. *Hermeticall Phyſick*, or the way to preſerve and reſtore health, by *Henry Nollius* Chymiſt, and Engliſhed by *Henry Vaughan*, Gent.

New Additions to the Catologue of Books Printed for *Humphrey Moseley* at the *Princes Armes* in St. *Paul's* Church-yard.

Various Historys, with Curious Discourses in Humane Learning, &c.

198 NEro *Cæsar*, or Monarchy Depraved, an Historicall work dedicated to the Duke of Buckingham, Lord High Admirall, by *Edmond Bolton.*

199. The Diet of the Diseased, divided into three Books, by Doctor *James Hart.*

200. The History of Ireland, from the yeare 1584. untill 1626. by Sir *James Perrot.*

201. Essaies by Sir *Charls Cornwallis* Junior, Knight.

202. The Mirror of Minds, or *Barclay's Icon Animorum*, Englished by *Thomas May*, Esq;

203. The works of *Caius Crispus Salustius*, Containing *Cataline's* Conspiracy; The Warre of *Iugurth*, and other rare Pieces, Englished by *William Crosse*, Gent.

204. Ld *Bacons* 3 speeches, Concerning the *Post-Nati*, The *Naturalization* of the Scotch in *England*, The Union of the Laws of the Kingdoms of *Engl.* and *Scotland.*

205. *Helvici Colloquia Familiaria Notis.*

206. The younger Brothers Advocate, or a Line or Two for younger Brothers, by *Champianus Northtonus.*

207. Two Letters of the Noble and Learned Marquesse, *Virgilii Malvezzi*, Translated out of Italian with some Observations Annexed seasonable for these times, by Mr. *Thomas Powell.*

208. Mr. *Howels Tumulus, Thalamus*, Two Poems, the first an Elegy upon *Edw.* Late Earl of *Dorset*, the second an Epithalamium to the Lord Marquesse of *Dorchester.*

209. Mr. *Howels* Parables Reflecting on the Times,

210. *Posselius Dialogues Engl. Lat.* by *Edmund Rives* B.D. and Instructor in all the Originall Tongues.

211. An Introduction into the Greek Tongue, most

B plainy

plainly delivering the principall matters of the Grammar thereof, Composed for their sakes, who understand not Latin, and yet are desirous to have Competent knowledge in that Language, by *Edmund Reeve* B. D. Instructor in all the Originall Tongues.

212. The Rules of the Latin Grammar Construed, which were omitted in the Book called *Lillies* Rules, and the Syntaxis Construed by *Edmund Reeve* B. D. Instructor in all the Originall Tongues.

213. An History of the late Warres, and other state affairs of Christendome, beginning with the King of *Swethlands* entrance into *Germany*, and continuing to the year, 1640. written in Italian by *Gualdo Priorato* and Englished by the Right Honourable *Henry* Earl of *Monmouth*.

214. *Ragguagli di Parnasso*; or Advertisements from *Parnassus*, written in Italian by that famous Roman; *Trajano Bocalini*, and put into English by the Right Honourable *Henry* Earl of *Monmouth*.

215. Politick Discourses written in Italian, by *Paul Paruta*, Gentleman of *Venice*, and Englished by the Right Honourable *Henry* Earl of *Monmouth*.

216. A Compleat History of the Lives and Reigns of *Mary* Queen of *Scotland*, and of her Son and Successor *James* the sixth, King of *Scotland*, and of Great *Brittain*, *France* and *Ireland*; The first (of ever blessed Memory) by *William Sanderson* Esq;

217. Letters to severall Persons of Honour, written by *John Donne*, sometime Dean of St. *Paul's*, London, Published by His Son.

218. A brief Description of the whole World describing the Monarchies Empires, and Kingdomes of the same with their Academies, by the Most Reverend Father in God, *George Abbot*, Late Arch-Bishop of *Canterbury*.

219. Observations on the united Provinces, and the state

ſtate of *France*, by Sir *Thomas Overbury.*

220. *Reliquiæ Wottonianæ*, or a Collection of Lives, Letters, Poems, with Characters of ſundry Perſonages, and other Incomparable Pieces of Language, and Art by the Curious pencill of the ever Memorable, Sir *Hen. Wotton* K[t], late Provoſt of *Eaton* Coll.

221. *Ducis Buckinghami in Ream Inſulam Expeditio: Authore Edwardo Domino Herbert, Barone de Cherbury. quam ſublici Juris fecit Timotheus Balduinus, LL. Doctor, è. Coll. omn. Anim. apud Oxonienſes Socius.*

222. Practicall Arithmetick in whole Numbers in Fractions, and Decimalls, fitted to the underſtanding of any Reaſonable Capacity, and very uſefull either for Gentlemen, Merchants, or Tradeſmen, by *Richard Rawlins* Profeſſor thereof in great *Yarmouth.*

Sermons with ſome Tracts in Divinity.

223. GOD ſave the King, a Sermon preached in St. *Pauls* Church, *March* 27th. 1639. By *Henry Valentine*, Doctor in Divinity.

224. *Noah's* Dove, or a Prayer for the peace of *Jeruſalem*, a Sermon by *Henry Valentine*, D.D.

225. Four Sea Sermons with Prayers, at the annuall meeting of the Trinity Company in the Pariſh Church of *Deptford*, by *Henry Valentine*, D. D.

226. The Merchants Manuall of Devotions, by Doctor Loe.

227. A Sermon called Arrierban, preached before the Military Company, by Dr. *Everard.*

228. Gages Recantation Sermon, Preached in Saint *Paul's* Church, called the Tyranny of Satan, who had been a Romiſh Prieſt 38. years.

229. A Sermon againſt murder, occaſioned by the Maſſacre of the Proteſtants, in the Dukedome of *Savoy*; by *William Towers*, B. D.

230. The Saints Expectation and Reward, a Sermon

at the Funerall of Mr. *Thomas Wiborough*, by *Michael Thomas*, Minister of *Stockden* in *Shropshire*.

231. Selfe Examination required in every one, for the worthy receiving of the Lords Supper, delivered in a Sermon preparatory to the Sacrament at S. *Martines* in the Fields, with a short Catechisme by *Dan. Cawdry.*

Choice Poems and Translations.

232. THe Shepheards Oracles in 10. Eclogues, by *Francis Quarls.*

233. The *Levites* Rvenge, or Meditations on the 19th of and 20th Chapter *Judges*, by *Robert Gomersal.*

234. Certain Psalms of *David*, Translated into English verse, by *Tho. May*, and *Tho. Carew*, Esquires.

235. Poems, Elegies Paradoxes, and Sonnets by Dr. *Henry* King, Lord Bishop of *Chichester.*

236. *Argalus* and *Parthenia*, written by *Francis Quarls*, illustrated with above thirty Pictures relating to the Story, never Printed before.

237. The Legend of Captain *Jones*, the first and second Parts.

238. The destruction of *Troy*, an Essay upon the second Book of Virgils Æneis, by *John Denham* Esq;

239. Poems, *viz.* 1. Miscellanies, 2. The Mistresse or Love Verses, 3. Pindarique Odes, 4. Davideis, or a sacred Poem of the Troubles of *David*, by *A. Cowley.*

Comedies and Tragedies.

240 BEn. *Johnsons* Works, The third Volum, containing 15. Masques at Court and elsewhere, also *Horaces* Art of Poetry Englished.
The English Grammar.
Timber or Discoveries,
Under woods, Consisting of diverse Poems.
The Magnetick Lady. A Tale of a Tub.
The sad Shepheard, or a Tale of Robbin hood.
Mortimers Fall.

24. The

241. The Devil is an Asse, by *Ben. Johnson.*

242. The Temple of Love, a Masque at *White-Hall* on Shrove-Tuesday, 1634. by Sir *W. Davenant*, Knight

243. *Brittania Triumphans*, a Masque at *White-Hall* on Twelfnight, 1637. by Sir *William Davenant*, Knight.

244. *Luminalia*, or the festivall Light, a Masque at Court on Shrove-Tuesday night, 1637. by Sir *William Davenant*, Knight.

245. *Salmacida Spolia*, A Masque at *White-Hall* on Tuesday, 21th of *January* 1639. by Sir *W. Davenant* Kt.

246. The Widdows Tears, a Comedy by *G. Chapman.*

247. May Day, a Comedy written by *George Chapman.*

248. Lodowick Sforza, Duke of *Millaine*, a Tragedy by *Robert Gomersall.*

249. Rule a Wife and have a Wife, a Comedy, by *Francis Beamont*, and *John Fletcher.*

250. *Rollo* Duke of *Normandy*, a Tragedy, by *Francis Beamont*, and *John Fletcher.*

251. The Knight of the Burning Pestle, a merry Comedy by *Francis Beamont* and *John Fletcher.*

252. Albumazer, a Comedy presented before the Kings Majesty at Cambridge, by the Gentlemen of Trinity Colledge, newly Revised and Corrected by a very speciall hand.

253. A Mad World my Masters, A Comedy written by *Thomas Midleton*, Gent.

254. Revenge for Honour, a Tragedy by *G. Chapman.*

255. The Spanish Gipsies, a Tragy Comedy, by *Thomas Middleton*, and *William Rowley*, Gent.

256. *Appius* and *Virginia*, a Tragedy by *John Webster*

New and Excellent Romances, lately Printed.

257 ARiana in two parts, Translated out of French and presented to My Lord *Chamberlaine*, with severall Additions.

258. The *Romant* of *Romants*, or the Love and Arms

of the Greek Princes, Tranſlated out of French.

259. *Aſtrea*, A Romance written in French, by *Meſſire Honore d' Urfe*, Tranſlated by a Perſon of quality; The firſt Part.

260. *Aſtrea*, A Romance the ſecond Part, written in French by *Meſſire Honore d' Urfe*, Tranſlated by the ſame Pen.

261. *Aſtrea*, A Romance the third and laſt Part, written in French by *Meſſire Honore d' Urfe*, Tranſlated by the ſame pen.

262. *Clelia*, An Excellent New Romance the firſt part written in French, by the Exquiſite Pen of *Monſieur de Scudery*, Governour of *Noſtredame de la Gard* Tranſlated by a Perſon of quality, The firſt Part.

263. *Clelia*, An Excellent New Romance, The ſecond Part, written in French by the Exquiſite Pen of *Monſieur de Scudery*, Governour of *Noſtredame de la Garde*, Tranſlated by the ſame hand.

264. *Clelia*, An Excellent New Romance, The third Part, written in French by the Exquiſite Pen of *Monſieur de Scudery*, Governour of *Noſtredame de la Garde*, Tranſlated by the ſame hand.

265. *Hymens Præludia*, or Loves Maſter-Piece, being The firſt Part of that ſo much admir'd *Romance*, Entituled *Cleopatra*, written by the Author of *Caſſandra*, Originally in French, and now Rendred into Engliſh, by *Robert Loveday*, Gent.

266 *Hymens Præludia*, or Loves Maſter-piece, being the Second Part of *Cleopatra*, Tranſlated out of French by *Robert Loveday*, Gent.

767. *Hymens Præludia*, or Loves Maſter-piece, being the Third Part of *Cleopatra*, Tranſlated out of French by *Robert Loveday*, Gent.

268. *Hymens Præludia*, or Loves Maſter-piece, being the Fourth Part of *Cleopatra*, Tranſlated out of French

269. *Hymens Præludia*, or Loves Maſter-piece, being the

the Fifth Part of *Cleopatra*, Translated out of French

270.*Hymens Præludia*, or Loves Master-piece, being the Sixth Part of *Cleopatra*, Translated out of French.

271.*Hymens Præludia*, or Loves Master-piece, being the Seventh Part of *Cleopatra*, Translated out of French.

272. *Hymens Præludia*, or Loves Master-piece, being the Eighth Part of *Cleopatra*, Translated out of French.

273. *Hymens Præludia*, or Loves Master-piece, being the Ninth Part of *Cleopatra*, Translated out of French.

274. *Hymens Preludia*, or Loves Master-piece, being the Tenth Part of *Cleopatra*, Translated out of French.

275.*Hymens Præludia*, or Loves Master-piece, being the Eleventh Part of *Cleopatra*, Translated out of French.

276. *Hymens Præludia*, or Loves Master-piece, being the Twelfth and last Part of *Cleopatra*, Translated out of French.

277. The Life of a Satyricall Puppy, called *Nim*, who worrieth all those Satyrists he knows, and barks at the rest by *W. D.*

Books lately Printed.

278. GLossographia or a *Dictionary*, interpreting all hard Words, whether Hebrew, Greek, Latin, Italian, Spanish, French, &c. as are now used in our Refined English Tongue: also the Tearms of Divinity, Law, Physick, Mathematicks Heraldry, War, Musick, and Architecture, by *Thomas Blount*, of the Inner Temple Barrester.

279. *Medici Catholicon*, or a Catholick Medicine for the Diseases of Charity, by *J. Collop*, D[r] in Physick.

280. *Poesis Rediviva*, or Poetry Revived by *John Collop*, Doctor in Physick.

281. *Mantuans Eslogues*, Englished by *Thomas Harvey*.

Books lately Printed.

282. A Divine Psalm or Song, wherein predestination is Vindicated by *John Davis*, 4°.

283. Entertainment of Solitarinesse, with Meditations and Prayers, by Sir *R. Tempest*, K[t] & Baronet, 12°.

284. Doctor *Valentines* private Devotions, with Letanies and Prayers for Morning and Evening, Rendred into Welch, by *G. L.* for his Countries good.

285. A Discourse of the Knowledge of Beasts, wherein all that hath been said for, against their Ratiocination, is examined by *Monsieur de la Chambre*, Counsellor to the King of *France*, and his Physician in ordinary, Englished by a Person of quality.

286. The siege of *Antwerp*, written in Latin by *Famianus Strada*, Englished by *Thomas Lancaster*, Gent.

287. Deserving Favorite, a Tragy Comeay, by *Lodowick Carlell*, Esquire, Presented before the King and Queens Majesty, with great Applause.

288. Two New Playes; the Fool would be a Favorite, or the Discreet Lover: 2 *Osmond* the great Turk, or the Noble Servant, by *Lodowick Carlell*, Esquire.

289. Two New Playes, 1. More dissemblers besides Women, 2. Women beware Women, by *Thomas Middleton*, Gent.

290. No Wit, No Help, like a Womans, a Comedy by *Thomas Middleton*, Gent.

291. Reflextions upon *Mounsieur des Cartes*, Discourse of a Method, for well Guiding of Reason, and discovery of Truth in Sciences, 8°.

292. Two Assize Sermons, Preached at *Bridgnorth*, for the County of *Salop*, in the year 1657 by *Mich. Thomas*, Rector of *Stockden* in the same County.

293. Of Peace, and Contentment of Mind, written by *Peter du Moulin* the Son, D. D.

294 A

Books lately Printed.

294. A Week of Soliloquies and Prayers, with a Preparation for the Holy Communion, by *Peter du Moulin*, the Son to Doctor *Moulin*.

295. A New Catalogue of the Dukes, Marqueſſes, Earls, Viſcounts, Barons, Baronets, Knights of the *Bath*, &c. with the times and places of their Creation.

296. God Incarnate, ſhewing that Jeſus Chriſt is the Onely and Moſt High God, in four Books, Containing Animadverſions, on Dr *Luſhingtons* Commentary on the Epiſtle to the *Hebrews*, by *Edmund Porter*, late of St. *John's* Colledge, *Camb. Prebend* of *Norwich*.

297. *Trin-unus-Deus*, or the Trinity and Unity of God, aſſerted againſt the Errors and Hereſies of the fifth Monarchy Men and others, by *Edmumd Porter*, late of St. *John's* Coll. *Camb. Prebend* of *Norwich*.

298. *Sabbatum*, or the Myſtery of the Sabbath diſcovered, ſhewing the Doctrine of the Sabbath, the meaning of the fourth Commandement, and of our Chriſtian Sunday, by *Edmund Porter*, late of St, *John's* Coll. *Camb. Prebend* of *Norwich*.

299. *Excommunicatio Excommunicata*, or a Cenſure of the Presbyterian Cenſures, and Proceedings in the Claſſis at *Mancheſter*, by *Nicholas Moſeley*, Eſq;

300. Love and War, a Tragedy by *Thomas Meriton*.

301. *Pierides*, or the Muſes Mount Poems, by *Hugh. Crompton*, Gent.

302. A Diſcourſe of the Empire of Germany, and the Election of the King of the Romans, by *James Howell* Eſq;

303. The Paſſion of *Dido* for *Æneas*, as it is incomparably expreſt in the fourth Book of Virgill, Tranſlated by *Edmund Waller*, and *Sidney Godolphin*, Eſquires.

304. Royall Pſalms, or Soliloquies of *Don Antonio*, King of *Portugall*, wherein the Sinner Confeſſeth his ſinnes, and imploreth the Grace of God, Tranſlated

Books lately Printed.

into Engliſh by *Baldwin* St. *George*, Gent.

305. The Life of *Adam*, written in Italian by *Gio Franciſco, Loredano*, a Venetian Nobleman, and Rendred into Engliſh by *J. S.*

306. *Barkers* delight, or the Art of Angling, diſcovering many Rare ſecrets, both for Catching and Dreſſing of Fiſh, by *Thomas Barker*, an Ancient Practitioner, with Additions.

307. Pearls of Eloquence, or the School of Complements, Deſcribing Beauty, Vertue, Love and Eloquence, Compoſed for young Ladyes & Gentlewomen

308. *Cheiragogia Heliana*, a Manuduction to the Philoſophers Magicall Gold, with *Zoroaſters* Cave, and the famous Catholick Epiſtle of *John Pontanus*, upon the minerall fire, by *Geo. Thor.* Aſtromagus.

309. *Chymia Cœleſtis*, Drops from Heaven, or pious Meditations and Prayers, on ſeverall places of Scripture, by *Ben. Parry*, Gent.

310. The Scarlet Gown, or the Hiſtory of the Lives of all the Preſent Cardinalls of *Rome*, written in Italian, and Engliſhed by *Hen. Cogan*, Gent. with an Addition of the Life of the Preſent Pope.

311. The laſt Remains of Sir *John Suckling*, being a full Collection of all his Poems and Letters ſo long Expected, and never till now publiſhed, with the Approbation of his noble and deareſt Friends.

312. The Life of the Renowned *Nicholas Claudius*, Fabricius Lord of Peireske, Senator of the Parliament at *Aix*, written by the Learned *Petrus Gaſſendus*, Profeſſor of the Mathematicks, to the King of *France*.

313. The ſtate of Chriſtendom, or a moſt Exact and Curious diſcovery, of many ſecret Paſſages and hidden Myſteries of the times, by the Renowned Sir *Henry Wotton* Knight, late Provoſt of *Eaton* Colledge.

Books lately Printed.

314. The Hiſtory of Philoſophy, the firſt Volume, Illuſtrated with diverſe figures of the Philoſophers, by *Thomas Stanley*, Eſq;

315. The Hiſtory of Philoſophy, the ſecond Volume, Illuſtrated with diverſe figures of the Philoſophers, by *Thomas Stanley*, Eſq;

316. The Hiſtory of Philoſophy, the third and laſt Volume, Illuſtrated with diverſe figures of the Philoſophers, by *Thomas Stanley*, Eſq;

317. The ſecret Miracles of Nature, in four Books written by that Famous Phyſician, *Lævinus Lemnius*, and Tranſlated into Engliſh.

318. A Compendious Hiſtory of the Sweeds, Goths and Vandalls, and other Northern Nations, by *Olaus Magnus*, Arch-Bp of *Vpſall*, & Metropolitan of *Sweden*.

319. The Hiſtory of the World, or an account of Time, Compiled by the Learned *Dionifius Petavius*, and continued by others to the year 1659. with a Geographicall deſcription of the World.

320. *Orbis Miraculum*, or the Temple of *Solomon*, decyphering all its famous Buildings, the pompous worſhip of the Jews, and all other, Their Rites and Ceremonies, by *Samuell Lee*.

321. A True and Exact Hiſtory of the Iſland of *Barbados*, Illuſtrated with a Map thereof, and the Principall Trees and Plants there in their due proportions and ſhapes, with the Ingin that makes the Sugar, and all other Circumſtances Cut in Copper, written by *Richard Ligon*, Gent.

322. Lectures upon *Geneſis*, &c. delivered at Saint *Paul's*, & St *Giles* Cripple gate, by that Reverend Father in God, *Lancelot Andrews*, late Lord Biſhop of *Winchester*, with an Epiſtle of Mr. *Peires* before it.

323. Things

Books lately Printed.

323. Things New and Old, or a Storehouse of Similies, Sentences, Allegories, Apothegmes, &c. Divine, Morall, & Politicall, with their Applications, Collected from the Writings & Sayings of the Learned in all Ages, to this present, by *John Spencer*.

324. Mosaicall Philosophy, grounded upon the Essentiall truth, or Eternall Sapience, written in Latin, and afterwards thus Rendred into English, by *Robert Fludd*, Esq; and Doctor of Physick.

325. A Compleat History of the Life and Reign of King *Charls* the First, from His Cradle to His Grave, Collected and written by *William Sanderson*, Esq;

326. The Commentaries of Sir *Francis Vere*, being divers pieces of Service, wherein he had Command, as at the Battell of Newport, and the Siege of Ostend, written by himselfe, and Published by *William Dillingham*, D. D.

327. Ayres and Dialogues, (to be sung to the *Theorbo Lute*, or Basse-Viol) by *John Gamble*.

328. The Vanity of Judiciary Astrology, or Divination by the Stars, written in Latin, by that Great Scholar, and Mathematician; the Illustrious *Petrus Gassendus*, Mathematicall Professor to the King of *France*, Englished by a Person of quality.

329. The Parable of the Tares, expounded and applied in ten Sermons, Preached before King *Charls* by *Peter Heylin*, D. D. To which are added three other Sermons, by the same Author.

330. Θεάνθρωπος, or God-Man, being an Exposition on part of the first Chapter of Saint *John*'s Gospell, Divinely handling the Divinity and Humanity of Jesus Christ, proving Him to be God and Man, &c. By that Reverend Divine, *John Arrowsmith*, D. D. late Master of Trinity Coll. *Cambridge*.

Books

Books now in the Presse, and to be Printed.

331 THe Universall History of *Monsieur d' Aubigne*, Comprized in three Tomes, beginning from the peace, between all the Christian Princes, and from the year 1550. To the pacification of the third Warre.

332. Sir *Charls Cornwallis* his Negotiation, as Leiger Ambassador for *Spain*, containing many secret Mysteries of State and Government, never before Published.

333. A discovery of the Hollanders trade of Fishing, and their Circumventing us therein, with a means how to make profit of the fishing, by which they have made, and yet do reap so great a benefit, by Sir *William Munson*, Knight, sometimes Vice Admirall of *England*.

334. *Clelia*, an Excellent New Romance, the fourth Volume, written in French by the Exquisite Pen of *Monsieur de Scudery*, Governour of Nostredame, *de la Garde*, Translated by a Person of quality.

335. The Grand *Scipio*, an Excellent new Romance, Translated by a Person of quality.

336. A perfect Collection or Catalogue of all Knights Batchelaurs made by King James since his comming to the Crown of England. Faithfully extracted out of the Records by *J. P.* Somerset Herald, A devout servant of the Royall Line.

337. The Manner of ordering Fruit trees, by the *Sieur le Gendre Curate* of *Henonville*, treating of Nurseries, Wall-Fruits, Hedges of Fruit Trees, Dwarf-Trees, High-Standers, &c. Translated at the Request of severall Persons of Honour.

338. A Realtion of the Captivity of *Sieur Emanuel d' Arand*, describing the miseries, Wiles, and Finesses of the Slaves and Pirates of *Algiers*, with the Conquests of Barbarossa in *Affrica*, &c. Englished by *J. W*

339. *Fas-.*

339. *Faſciculus Poematum et Epigramatum Miſcelaneorum Authore Johanne Dome,* D. D. and Engliſhed by *Jaſper Maine,* Doctor in Divinity

340. *Poemata Græca & Latina Authore Gulielmo Cartwright,* C. C. Oxon.

These Books I purpoſe to Print, Deo Volente.

341. HEſperides, or the Muſes Garden, ſtored with the choiceſt Flowers of Language and Learning, wherein grave and ſerious minds may taſt the Fruits of Philoſophy, Hiſtory and Coſmography with the ſweets of Poetry, and the ceremonious Courtier, the paſſionate Amouriſt with his admired Lady, may gather Rarities ſuitable to their fancies, by *John Evans,* Gent.

342 Diſquiſitions upon the Nativity of Our Saviour Jeſus Chriſt, by the Honourable Sir *Iſaac Wake.*

343. The expedition of the Duke of *Buckingham,* into the Iſle of *Rhee*, written in Latin by the Right Honourable *Edward* Lord *Herbert* of *Cherbury,* &c. and now Engliſhed.

344. The Anatomy of ſenſuall and prophane Love, written in Italian by *Mateo Palma,* and Engliſhed by *J. S.*

345. *Nicholas Flammell,* his Expoſition of his Hieroglyphicall figures, with the ſecret Book of *Artephius,* and the Epiſtle of *John Pontanus,* concerning the Philoſophers ſtone, with Additions upon the ſame ſubject, by *Synetius* that moſt Learned and Famous Græcian *Abbot,* never printed before.

346. *Brittains Ida,* written by that Renowned Poet, *Edmund Spencer,* Publiſhed by Sir *Kenelm Digby* Knight.

347. A Grammar Lecture, with Elegies written by *Francis Beaumont,* Gent.

348. A

These Books I purpose to Print, Deo Volente.

348. A Discourse touching peace with *Spain*, and retaining the *Netherlands* in protection, written by Sir *Walter Raleigh* Knight, presented to his Majesty.

349. A Discourse of the Warre of *Germany*, with the Lord Chancellour *Bacons* Petition, and submission to the House of Peeres.

350. *Andrea Palladio*, his four Books of Architecture, treating of private Buildings, High-wayes, Piazzas, Exercising Places and Temples, Translated out of Italian by *H. L.* Esquire.

351. Letters and others pieces of that Excellent French Wit, *Monsieur Theophilee*, Englished by *J. W.*

352. The Incestuous Innocent, a true story.

353. *Dominus Deus*, or the divine Prerogative, containing 21 Sermons, preached upon the fifth Chapter of *Deuteronomy*, by that late Eminent Divine, Mr. *Josias Shute*, B. D. and above three and thirty years Rector of St. *Mary Woolnoth* in Lombard-street, *London*.

354. The Spring Garden of Witt and Love, for generous Spirits to walke in, with the Art of woing and complementing: with a faire Prospect into the Garden of the Muses, as Poems, Epigram and Songs, with other Ravishing delights in the Art of Poesies, for the further accomplishment of the Practitioner there is a Rapsodie of Similitudes, Emblems, Devices, Charracters, Jests, Jeeres, &c. with Exquisite silent Dispatches of the best A la mode Letters. Together with a short Essay of a new invented Ditionary for the english Tongue. A work never before published, but now Phænix like raised out of the Ashes of the Incomperablest Modern Authors, and out of the choicest Manuscripts of the Witts of these times, for a Generall good.

Theſe Books I purpoſe to Print, Deo volente.

355. *Mercurius Academicus*, Containing moſt high and quaint expreſſions of Language, Conceited youthfull Poems, Letters, with amorous diſcourſes for Table talk, and other moſt Gentile Accompliſhments.

356. The Hiſtory of *Anaxander* and *Orazia*, by Sir *Deboys Robert*, A new Romance Tranſlated into Engliſh.

357. *Clorinda*, A new Romance, Tranſlated out of French.

358. *Plutoſophia*, or the Art of Memory, as well Naturall as Artifitiall, written in Italian by that Learned Maſter in this Art, *Philippo Geſvaldo*, and Tranſlated into Engliſh.

359. The Hiſtory of Thamberlaine the great.

360. *Davideis ſive Hiſtoria Davidis Regis Libris quatuor Scripta*, *p.* Abraham Cowley.

361. Severall Sermons on the ninth Chapter of St. *Lukes* Goſpell, from the 28th. to the 37th. Verſe, by *John Arrowſmith*, D. D. late Maſter of Trinity Colledge in *Cambridge*.

362 Severall Sermons on the fifth Chapter of the firſt Epiſtle to the *Theſſalonians*, the 6th. Verſe, by *John Arrowſmith*, D. D. late Miniſter of Trinity Colledge *Cambridge*.

363. Mr. *Edward Wright* Revived, or Mr. *Edward Wrights* Projection, ſo illuſtrated both by Inſtrumentall and Logarithmicall operations, as it may moſt eaſily be underſtood by the meaneſt Capacity, together with diverſe Mapps, and deſcriptions of ſeverall Ports, Iſlands, and places in the Eaſt-Indies, by *Robert Jager*, Gent. of *Sandwich* in Kent.

APPENDIX

Poems from MS Don d 55

(Original page size 239 x 170 cms.)

To the Queene ([illegible])

Madam

(If yor Matie: had lived in those times, which sacrificed to the
unn, and Moone, and of each glorious Creature made a new
eitie, as the admiration of yor Sacred Person had supplyed
em with a more excusable Idolatry: Wee could not Incense
ve bin more worthy yor Alter, then the Odor of his Maties
eroicke Deeds: And though the Court, and Universities have
o other matter of their Song: yet if yor Matie please to listen
hat Eccho the Countrey returns to soe loud a Prayse, Wee
all likewise teach the Woods to sound yor Royall Name, and
ll how greate a portion of our present happiness is owinge
those Divine Graces, wherein all the private desires of our
overaigne being accomplished, hee is wholy att leasure to con-
nferr Felicitie on others: For Continence (soe greate a
iracle in the Vigor of Youth and Royaltie) Wee number
mongst the meanest of his Virtues, whose Bed soe highly
owned with Blood and Beautie, presents him with all, that
tiquitie and Youth cann give: Nor is our neighbour Kingdome
ss requited for the Light it first shewed you, in that his
Matie: injoying the fayrest parte, is soe well content with a Title
the rest of France: But wee looke not on yor Matie as the Cause
ly, but as the Pledge of our Securitie: For as Heaven
reatens a Deluge of all Calamities upon a Land condemned
to the State of Warr: Soe may our Nation well expect the
ntrary Blessings being chosen for the Seate of Love: A Love
famous, fruitfull, and religiously observed betwixt yor most
cellent Maties that like the sacred Oyle, wherewith the Royall
[illegible] perfumed his Song of Fraternall Amitie) diffused [illegible]

from

from the Head downe to the Skirts the meanest of your
People) It affords us all with the Joy of soe Noble a President:
Nor doth Heaven seeme less to acknowledge this Pietie, still bin
yo: Kingdomes togeather with soe many hopefull Knotts, that w
are now confident noe other Streame of Blood, shall ever
divide the Power of this happy Island: For which Graces, yo
Matie: is not named amongst Us without Prayers, that when y
shall have exceeded the Common Fate of Humane Condition, no
less in time, then in Glory, You may receive that Welcome
amongst the Glad Angells, To which the Resemblance both of th
Brightnes, and Innocence gives you alreadie soe fayre a
Title

Yo: Maties

The Misers Speech in a Maske:/

alls of this Mettall slack'd Atlanta's pace
nd on the Amarous youth bestow'd the race
enus the Nimphs mind, measuring by her owne
vhome the rich spoyles of Citties overthrowne
ad prostrated to Mars, could well advise
h'adventurous Lover, how to gayne the prize:
or less may Jupiter to Gold ascribe
vhoe when hee turn'd himselfe into a Bribe
vhoe can blame Danae, or the Brazen Towre
hat they withstood not the Almightie Showre:
ever till then did Love, make Jove putt on
 forme more bright, and noble then his owne
or were it Just, would hee resume that Shape
hat slacke Devotion, should his Thunder scape
was not revenge, for greiv'd Apollo's wrong
hose Asses Eares upon dull Mydas hung;
ut fond Repentance of his happie Wish
ecause his Meate grew Mettall, like his dish
Vould Bacchus bless mee soe, I'de constant hold
nto my Wish, and dye Creatinge Gold:/

On the Freindshipp betwixt Zacharissa and Amorett

Tell mee Lovely Loving Payre
why soe kinde, and soe severe
why soe carelesse of our Care
onely to yo:r selves soe deare.
By this cunning change of hearts
You the power of Love controwle
while the Boyes deluded Darts
Can arrive att neither Sowle.

For in vaine to eithers Breast
Still beguiled Love does come
Where hee finds a forreigne Guest
Neither of yo[r] Hearts at home.

Debtors thus with like designe
When they never meane to pay
That they may the Lawe decline
To some ffreinds make all away
Not the Silver Doves that fly
yoak't in Cythareas Carr
Not the wings that lift soe high
And convey her Sonne soe farr;

Are soe lovely, sweete, and fayre
Or doe more enoble Love
Are soe choycely match't a payre
Or with more consent doe move./

On the heade of a Stagg

Soe wee some Antique Heros strength
Learne by his Launces, weight, and Length
As theis vast Beams expresse the Beast
Whose shadowd Brows alive they drest
Such game, while yet the World was new
The mightie Nimrod did pursue
What Huntsman of our feeble race
Or Dogs dare such a Monster chase
Resembling, with each blow hee strikes
The charge of a whole Troope of Pikes
Oh fertile head, which every yeare
Could such a crop of wonder beare
The teeming earth did never bring
Soe soone, soe hard, soe huge a thing

which

hich might it never have byn cast
ch yeares growth added to the last
heis loftie Branches had supplyd
he earths bold Sonns prodigious pride
eaven with theis Engines had byn scald
hen Mountaines heapd on Mountayns fayld. /

The Storie of Phebus, and Daphne applyed. /

irsis a youth of the Inspired Trayne
ayre Sacharissa lovd, but lovd in vayne
Phebus sung the noe less amarous Boy
Daphne shee as lovely, and as coy
th numbers hee the flying Nimph pursues
th numbers such as Phebus selfe might use
ch is the chase, when Love and Fancie leads
cragge Mountaines, and through flowrie Meads
vext to testifie the Lovers care
forme some Image of his cruell fayre
gd with his furie, like a wounded Deere
those hee fledd, and now approaching neere
reachd the Nimph with his harmonious Lay
hom all his Charms could not inclyne to stay
t what hee sung in his Immortall strayne
ough unsuccessfull) was not sung in vayne
(but the Nimph that should redress his wrongs)
tends his passion, and approves his Song:
Like Phebus thus acquiring unsought prayse
Hee catchd att Love, and filld his arms with Bayse.

Of the misreport of her being Painted

when a Sorte of Wolves infest the night
h their wilde howlings, att fayre Cynthias Light
noyse may chase sweete Slumber from our Eyes
never reach the M[rs] of the Skyes
vexed Servants blame those envious tongues
with the news of Sacharillas wrongs)

Call

Call Love to witnes, that noe painted fire
Cann scorch men soe, or kindle such desire
Whilst unconcern'd shee, seemes mov'd noe more
With this new malice then our Love before
But from the height of her greate minde lookes downe
On both our passions, without smile, or frowne
Soe little care of what is done belowe
Hath the bright Dame, whome Heaven affecteth soe.
Paynts her tis true, wth the same hand which spreads
Like glorious colours through the flowrie Meads
When lavishing Nature wth her best attire
Cloaths the gay Spring, the Season of desire
Paynts her tis true, and does her cheeks adorne
With the same Art, wherewth shee paynts the Morne
With the same Arte, wherewth shee guildeth soe
Those painted Clouds, which forme Thaumantias Bowe./

To Amorett.

Faire that you may truly knowe
What you unto Thirsis owe,
I will tell you how I doe
Sacharissa loves you

Joy salutes mee when I sett
My blest eyes on Amorett
But with wonder I am strooke
When I on the other looke

If sweete Amorett complaine
I have sense of all her paine
But for Sacharissa I
Doe not only greive but dye.

All that of my selfe is mine
Lovely Amorett is thine
Sacharissas Captive fayne
Would untie his yron chayne

nd those scorching Beames to shun
So thy gentle shadowe runn
If the Sowle had free Election
To dispose of her affection
I should not thus long have borne
Haughtie Sacharilla's Scorne
But tis sure some power above
Which controules our Will in Love.

If not Love, a strong desire
To Create and spread that fire
In my Breast) sollicites Mee
Beautious Amorett for thee
Tis Amazement more then Love
Which her radiant Eyes doe move:
If lesse splendour wayte on thine
Yet they soe benignly shine
I would turne my dazeled Sight
To behold their milder Light
But as hard 'tis to destroy
That high flame, as to enjoy:
Which how easily I may doe
Heaven (as easily scal'd) does knowe.

Amorett as sweete, and good
As the most delitious ffood.
Which but tasted does Impart
Light, and gladnes to the harte
Sacharilla's Beautie's Wyne
Which to Madnes doth encline
Such a Liquor as noe Brayne
That is Mortall can sustayne
Scarse can I to Heaven excuse
That devotion which I use
Unto that adored Dame
For 'tis not unlike the same
Which I thither ought to send
Soe that if it could take end
T would to Heaven it selfe bee due
To succeede her, and not you;
Whoe alreadie have of mee
All that's not Idolatrie
Which though not soe feirce a flame
Is longer like to bee the same

Then smile on mee, and I will prove
Wonder is shorter liv'd then Love

Songe

Behold the Brand of Beawtie tost
See how the motion does dilate the flame
Delighted Love his spoyles does boast
And triumph in this same
ffire to noe place confin'd.
Is both our wonder, and our feare
Moving the Minde
Like Lightning hurled through the Ayre.
High heaven the glorie does increase
Of all her shyninge Lamps, this artfull way
The Sunn in figures, such as these
Joyes with the Moone to play
To the sweete strayns they advance
which doe result from their owne Spheares
As the Nimphs dance
Moves with the numbers, which she heares. /

of Mrs Arden

Behold and listen, while the fayre
Breaks in sweete sounds the willing ayre
And with her owne breath, fanns the fire
Which her bright eyes doe first inspire
What reason cann that Love controule
which more then one way courts the Sowle.
See when a flash of lightning falls
On our abodes, the danger calls
ffor humane ayd, wch hopes the flame
To conquerr, though from heaven it came
But if the Winde with that conspire
Men strive not, but deplore the fire. /

To a Ladie from whome hee receiv'd a Silver Penn./

Madame

Intending to have tryed
The Silver favour which you gave
In Inke the Shining point I dyed.
And drench'd it in the Sable Wave
When greiv'd to bee soe foulie stayn'd
On you to mee, it thus Complayn'd:

Suppose you had deserv'd to take
ffrom her fayre hand, soe faire a Boone
Yet how deserved I to make
Soe ill a change, who ever woon
Immortall prayse for what I wrought
Instructed by her Noble thought.

I that expressed her commands
To mightie Lords, and princely Dames
Alwaies most welcome to their hands
Proud that I would record their names
Must now bee taught an humble stile
Some meaner Beawtie to beguile.

Soe I the wronged Penn to please
Make it my humble thankes expresse
Unto yo: Ladyship in these
And now tis forced to confesse
That your greate selfe, did nere indite
Nor that to one more noble write./

On a Brayde of divers Colours woven by Fowre Ladies.

Fowre twentie slender Virgins fingers twyne
This Curious Webb, where all their fancies shine
As Nature them, Soe they this shade have wrought
Soft as their hands, and various as their thoughts
Not Juno's Bird, when his fayre trayn's dispread
Hee wooes the Female to his painted bead
Noe not the Bowe, which soe adornes the Skyes
Soe glorious is, or boasts soe many dyes.

To A Ladie in Retirement

Sees not my Love how Time resumes
The glory which hee lent these flowres
Though none should taste their sweete perfumes
yet must they live, but some few howres
Time (what wee forbeare) devowres.

Had Hellen or the Egiptian Queene
Bin nere soe thriftie of their graces
Those Beawties must att length have been
The spoyle of Age, which finds out faces
In the most retired places.

Should some malignant Planett bring
A barren Drowght, or ceaseles Showre
Vpon the Autumne or the Springe
And spare us neither fruite, nor flowre
Winter would not stay an howre.

Could the resolve of Loves neglect
Preserve thee from the violation
Of Comming yeares, then more respect
Were due to soe devine a fashion
Nor would I, indulge my Passion.

Songe. /

y Lovelie dreame, where couldst thou finde
Shadows to counterfeit thy face
Colours of this glorious kinde
ome not from any mortall place. /

n Heaven it selfe thou sure wert drest
With that Angell like disguise
Thus deluded am I blest
And see my Joy with closed Eyes.

But ah this Image is too kinde
To bee other then a dreame
Cruell Sacharillas minde
Never put on that sweete extreame

Fayre dreame, if thou intendst mee grace
Change this heavenly forme of thine
Paint despisd Love, in this face
And make it to appeare like mine. /

Pale, Wann, and Meager let it looke
With a pittie moving Shape
Such as Wander by the Brooke
Of Lethe, or from Graves escape:

Then to that matchles Nymph appeare
In whose shape thou shinest soe
Softlie in her sleeping eare
With humble words expresse my woe.

Perhaps from greatnes, State, and pride
Thus surprized shee may fall
Sleepe does disproportion hide
And Death resembling, equalls all. /

Of the Ladie whoe cann Sleepe when shee Pleaseth

Noe wonder Sleepe from carefull Lovers flyes
To bathe himselfe in Sacharilla's Eyes
As fayre Astrea, once from Earth to Heaven
By Strife, and lowd Impietie was driven
Soe with our plaints offended, and our teares
Wise Somnus to that Paradis repayres;
Waytes on her Will, and Wretches does forsake
To Courte the Nimph, for whome those Wretches wake
More proud then Phebus of his Throane of Gold
Is the soft God, those softer Limbs to hold
Nor would exchange with Jove to hide the Skyes
In darkling Clowds, the power to close her Eyes,
Eyes which soe farr all other Lights controwle
They warme our mortall parts, but theis our Soule
Lett her free Spiritt, whose unconquerd breast
Hold such deepe quiett, and untroubled rest
Knowe that though Venus, and her Sonne should spare
Her rebell heart, and never teach her care
Yet Hymen may Inforce her Vigills keepe
And for another Joy, suspend her Sleepe./

Of her passing through a Crowd of People

As in old Chaos, Heaven, with Earth confus'd
And Starrs with rocks togeather crush'd, and bruis'd
The Sunn his Light, noe further could extend
Then the next Hill, which on his Shoulder lean'd
Soe in this throng bright Sacharilla far'd
Oppressed by those, who strove to bee her guard
As Shipps though never soe obsequious, fall
Fowle in a tempest, on their Admirall:

A greater favour this disorder brought
Unto her Servants, then their awfull thought
Durst entertaine, when thus compell'd, they prest
The yeilding Marble, of her snowy Breast
While Love insults, disguised in the Crowde
And welcome force of the unruly Crowde
Soe th'amarous Tree, while yet the ayre is calme
Just distance keepes, from his desired Palme
But when the Winde her ravisht branches throws
Into her Armes, and mingle all their Bows
Though loath hee seemes, her tender leaves to press
More loath hee is, that freindly storme should cease
From whose rude Bountie hee the double Use
Att once receives of Pleasure, and Excuse./

On my Lady Dorathy Sidneys Picture./

Such was Philocleas, such was Dorus flame
The matcles Sidney, that immortall frame
Of perfect Beautie, on twoe pillars plac't
Not his high fancie could one patterne, grac't
With such extreames of Excellencie compose
Wonders soe distant in one face disclose
Such chearefull modestie, such humble State
Moves certaine Love, but with as doubtfull Fate
As when beyond our greedie reach wee see
Inviting fruite on too sublime a tree
All the rich flowres, through his Arcadia found
Amaz'd wee see, in this one Garland bound
Had but this coppie which the Artist tooke
From that fayre picture, of that noble booke
Stood att Calanders, the brave freinds had Jarr'd
And rivalls made, the insuing storie marr'd
Just Nature first instructed by his thought
In his owne house thus practis'd what he taught
This glorious peice transcends what he could thinke
Soe much his Blood is nobler then his inke./

To vandike

Rare Artisan, whose pensill moves
Not our delight alone, but Loves
From thy Shopp of Beawtie wee
Slaves return'd that entred free
The heedles Lover does not knowe
Whose Eyes they are, that wound him soe
But confounded with thy Art
Requires her name, that has his heart
Another who did long refrayne
ffeels his old wounds, bleed fresh againe
With deare remembrance of that face
Where now hee reads new hopes of grace
Nor Scorne, nor crueltie does finde
But gladly suffers a false winde
To blowe the Ashes of despaire
From the reviving brand of Care
ffoole that forgetts her stubborne looke
This softnes from thy finger tooke
Strange that thy hand should not inspire
The Beawtie only, but the fire
Not the forme alone, and grace
But art, and power of a face
Mayst thou yet thy selfe aswell
As all the world beside excell
Soe thou th'unfeigned truth rehearse
That I may make it live in Verse
Why thou couldst not, att one assay
That face to after time convey
Which this admires, was it thy witt
To make her oft before thee sitt
Confess, and wee'le forgive thee this
ffor whoe would not repeate that bliss
And frequent sight of such a Dame
Buy with the hazard of his ffame
Yet whoe cann tax thy blameles skill
Though thy good hand, had fayled still
When natures selfe soe often erres
Shee for this many thousand yeares

s practis'd with much care
frame the race of women faire
t never could a perfect birth
roduce before, to grace the earth
hich waxed old, ere it could see
er that amaz'd thy art, and thee

But now 'tis done, ô let mee knowe
Where those immortall colours growe
That could this deathles peece compose
In Lillie, or the fading rose
Nee for this theft thou hast clym'd higher
Then did Prometheus for his fire./

In Answer to ye

What furie has provoak'd thy witt to dare
With Dyomed. to wound the Queene of Love
hy Mrs envy, or thy owne despaire
ot the Just Pallas in thy breast did move
Soe blinde a rage, with such a different fate
Hee honour won where thou hast purchas'd hate./

he gave assistance to his Troian foe
hou that wthout a rivall, thou mayst love
ost to the Beautie of this Ladie owe
hile after her, the gazing world does move
Canst not thou bee content to love alone
Or is thy Mrs not content with one.

st thou not reade of ffayrie Arthurs shield
hich but disclos'd amaz'd the weaker eyes
proudest foe, and won the doubtfull feild
o shall thy rebell witt, become her prize.
Should thy Iambicks swell into a booke
All were confuted wth one radiant looke.

aven her oblig'd, that plac't her in the Skyes
warding Phebus for inspiring soe
noble brayne, by likening to those eyes
ioyfull beames: But Phebus is thy foe
And neither ayds thy fancie, nor thy sight
Soe ill thou rym'st, against soe fayre a Light./

To my Lord Admirall of his late Sicknes and Recoverie

With Ioy like ours, the Thracian youth invade
Orpheus, returning from th Elisian Shade
Embrac'd the Heroe, and his stay Implore
Make it their publique suite, he would not more
Desert them soe, and for his Spouses sake
His vanisht Love, tempt the Lethæan Lake
The Ladies to the brightest of that time
Ambitious all his loftie bed to clyme
Their doubtfull hopes, with expectation feed
Whoe shall the fayre Euridice succeed
Euridice, for whome his numerous moane
Makes listning Trees, and salvadge mountains groane
Through all the ayre, his sounding strings dilate
Sorrowe like that, which toucht our hearts of late
Your pyning sicknes, and your restles paine
Att once the Land affecting, and the Mayne
When the glad newes that you were Admirall
Scarce through the Nation spread, 'twas fear'd by all
That our great Charles whose Wisdome shines in You
Would bee perplexed how to choose a new
Soe more then private, was the ioy and greife
That att the worst it gave our Soules releife
That in our age such sence of vertue liv'd
They ioy'd soe iustly, and soe iustly greiv'd
Nature her fayrest lights eclipsed seems
Herselfe to suffer in theis sharpe extreams
While not from thine alone, thy blood retires
But from those cheeks, which all the world admires
The stemm thus threatned and the sapp in thee
Droope all the branches of that noble tree
Their beautie they and wee our Love suspend
Nought cann our wishes save thy health intend
As Lillies overcharg'd with rayne, they bend
Their beautious heads, and with high Heaven contend
Hold thee within their snowy arms, and cry
Hee is too faultles, and too young to dye
Soe like Immortalls round about thee they
Sitt that they fright approaching death away
Whoe would not languish by soe fayre a trayne
To bee lamented and restor'd againe

thus withhold; what hastie Soule would goe
ough to the blest, ere young Adonis soe
ave Venus mourn'd, and with the pretious showres
her warme teares, cherish the springing flowres
e next supporte, fayre hope of yo:r greate Name
d Second pillar of that noble frame
y loss of thee, would not advantage have
ut steppe by steppe pursues thee to the Grave
n now relentles state, about to end
he Lyne which backwards doth soe farr extend
hat Antique stocke, which still the world supplies
ith bravest spirits, and with brightest Eyes
ince Phebus interposing bid mee say
uch stormes noe more shall shake that howse, but they
ike Neptune, and his Seaborne Neere Talbot
he shyning glories of the Land and Sea
With courage guard, and Beautie warme our age
And Lovers fill with like poetique rage./

To my Lord of Northumberland upon the deathe of his Ladie:/

this greate loss a Sea of teares is due
But the whole debt not to bee paid by you
harge not yo:r selfe with all, nor render vaine
hose showres the eyes of us yo:r Servants raine
hall greife contract the largenes of that hearte
n which nor feare, nor anger has a parte
ertue would blush if time should boast (w:ch dryes
ir sole child dead, the tender Mothers Eyes)
yo:r minds releife, where reason triumphs soe
Over all passions, that they nere could growe
Beyond their limitts in yo:r noble breast
To harme another, or impeach yo:r rest
This wee observ'd delighting to obey
ONE whoe did never from his greate selfe stray
whose mild example seemed to ingage
Th'obsequious Seas, and teach them not to rage
The brave Emilius his greate charge layd downe
The force of Rome, and state of Macedon)
n his lost Sonnes, did feele the cruell stroake
f changing fortune, and thus highly spoake:

Before Romes people wee did oft Implore
That if the Heavens had any ill in store
For yor Emilius, they would powre it ill
On his owne howse, and let you flourish still
You on the barren Seas my Lord have spent
Whole springs, and Summers to the publique Lent
Suspended all the pleasures of yor life
And shortned the short Joy of such a wife
For which yor Countreys more obliged then
For many lives of Old less happie Men
You that have sacrificed soe greate a parte
Of youth, and private bliss, ought to imparte
Your Sorrowe too, and give yor frinds a right
Aswell in yor affliction, as delight
Then with Emilian courage, beare this crosse
Since publique persons, only publique losse
Ought to afforde, and though her forme and youth
Her application to yor Will, and truth
That noble sweetnes, and that humble state
All snatcht away, by such a hastie Fate
Might give excuse to any common breast
With the hugh weight of soe iust greife opprest
Yet [illegible] let noe portion of yor life be stayn'd
With passion, but yor Character mainteyn'd
To the last acte; It is enough her Stone
May honour'd bee with Superscription
Of the sole Ladie, whoe had power to move
The Greate Northumberland to greive, and love.

To my Younge Lady Lucie Sidney.

Why came I soe untimely forth
Into a World, which wanting thee
Could entertaine us with noe worth
Or shadowe of felicitie
That time should mee soe farr remove
From that which I was borne to Love.

Yet fairest blossoms doe not slight
That age which you must knowe soe soone
The rosie morne resignes her light
And milder glorie to the Moone
And then what wonders shall you doe
Whose dawninge Beautie warns us soe

Hope waytes upon the flowrie prime
And Summer though it bee less gay
Yet is not look'd on as a time
Of declynation, or decay
ffor wth. a full hand it doth bring
All that was promis'd by the Springe./

To my Lord of Leicester

Not that thy trees of Penshurst groane
Oppressed with their timely loade
And seeme to make their silent moane
That their greate Lord, is now abroad
That to delight his taste, or Eye
Would spend themselves in fruite and dye.
Not that thy harmeles Deere repine
And thinke themselves unjustly slaine
By any other hand, then thine
Whose arrowes they would gladly stayne
Not nor thy ffreinds which hold too deare
That peace with ffrance which keepes thee there:
All these are less then that greate cause
Which now exacts yor: presence heere
Whereiu their meete the divers Lawes
Of publique, and domestique care
ffor one bright youth, or Nimph contends
And on yor: prudent choyce depends./
Not the bright sheild of Thetis Sonn
ffor which such sterne debate did rise
That the greate Aiax Telemon
Refus'd to live without the prize
Those Achaiv Peeres did more ingage
Then thee the gallants of our age.

That Beame of Beautie which begunn
To warme us soe, when thou wert heere
Now scorches like the radiant Sunn
When Syrius does first appeare
Oh fix this flame, and lett despaire
Redeeme the rest from endles care./

Att Penshurst./

Had Dorrothea liv'd, when mortalls made
Choyce of their Deities, this sacred Shade
Had held an Altar to the power that gave
The peace and glory which these Allies have
Embroydred soe with flowers, where shee stood
That it became a garden of a Wood
Whose presence has such more then humane grace
That it cann Civilize the rudest place
And beautie too, and order cann Impart
Where nature nere intended it, nor Art
The plants acknowledge this, and her admire
Not less then those of old did Orpheus Lyre
If shee sitt downe, with topps all towards her bow'd
They round about her into Arbours crow'd
Or if she walke in even rancks they stand
Like some well marshall'd and obsequious band
Amphion soe made stones, and Timber leape
Into faire figures from a confused heape
And in the Symetrie of her parts is found
A power like that of Harmonie in sound
Yee loftie Beeches tell this matchles Dame
That if togeather yee feed all on flame
It could not equalize the hundredth parte
Of what her eyes has kindled in my harte
Goe Boy and carve this passion on the barke
Of yonder tree, which stands the sacred marke
Of noble Sidneys birth when such
Such more then mortall-making starrs did shine
That there they cannot but for ever prove
The monument and pledge of humble Love
His humble Love, whose hopes shall nere rise higher
Then for a Pardon that hee dares admire./

Of the Danger his Ma:tie (being Prince) escaped att the Rode att Saint Andrews:/

ow had his Highnes bidd farewell to Spaine
nd reached the Spheare of his owne power the Mayne
vith Brittish bountie in his Shipp hee feasts
h' Hesperian Princes his amazed Guests
o finde that watry Wildernes exceede
he Entertainement of their greate Madrid
ealths to both Kings, attended with the roare
f Cannons eccho'd from the affrighted Shoare
vith lowde resemblance of his thunder prove
acchus the seede of cloude compelling Jove
hiles to his harpe devine Arion sings
he Loves and conquests of our Albion Kings
f the ffowrth Edward was his noble Song
ierce, goodly, valiant, beautifull, and young
ee rent the crowne from vanquish'd Henries head
ays'd the white rose, and trampled on the redd
ill Love triumphing on the Victors pride
rought Mars, and Warwicke to the vanquish'd side
eglected Warwicke, whose bold hand like ffate
ives, and resumes the Scepter of our State
voes for his Master, and with double shame
imselfe deluded, mocks the princely Dame
he Lady Bona, whome iust anger burns
nd forreigne Warr, with civill rage returns
h spare yo:r swords, where beautie is too blame
ove gave th' affront, and must repayre the same
When ffrance shall boast of her, whose conquering Eyes
ave made the best of English hearts their prize
ave power to alter the decree of ffate
nd change againe the Councells of our State
What the Prophetique Muse intends alone
To him it selfe that secrett wound is knowne
With the sweete sound of this harmonious Lay
About the keele delighted Dolphins play
Too sure a signe of Seas ensuing rage
Which must anon this royall Troope ingage
To whome soft sleepe seemes more secure, and sweete
Within the Towne comanded by our ffleete:

Those mighty Peeres plac'd in the Guilded Barge
Proud with the burden of soe brave a charge
With painted Oares the youth beginns to sweepe
Neptunes smooth face, and cleave the yeilding deepe
Which soone becomes the seate of sodaine Warr
Betwixt the Winde, and tide, that fiercely ~~fly~~ Jarr
As when a sorte of lustie Sheppards try
Their force att Football, care of Victorie
Makes them salute soe rudely breast to breast
That their encounter seems too rough for Jest
They ply their feete, and still the restles Ball
Tost too and froe, is urged by them all
Soe fares the doubtfull Barge twixt Tides, and winds
And like effects of their contention finds
Yet the bold Brittons still securely row'd
Charles, and his vertue was their sacred Load
Then which a greater pledge Heaven could not give
That the good Boate this tempest should outlive
But stormes increase, and now noe hope of grace
Among them shines, save in the Princes face
The rest resigne their courage, skill, and sight
To danger horrour, and unwelcome night
The gentle Vessell wont with state, and pride
On the smooth backe of Silver Thames to ride
Wanders astonisht through the angrie Mayne
As Titans Carr did while the golden rayne
Fild the young hand of his adventurous Sonne
When the whole world an equall hazard runn
To this of ours, the light of whose desire
Waves threaten now, as that was scarde by fire
The impatient Sea growes impotent, and raves
That (night assisting) his impetuous Waves
Should finde resistance from soe light a thing
These surges ruyne, those our safetie bring
Th'oppressed Vessell doth the charge abide
Only because assaild on every side
Soe men with rage and passion sett on fire
Trembling for haste impeach their madd desire
The pale Iberians had expird with feare
But that their wonder, did divert their care
To see the Prince with danger mov'd not more
Then with the pleasures of their Court before

dlike his courage seem'd, whome nor delight
uld soften, nor the face of Deathe affright
rot to the power of making tempests cease
as in that Storme, to have soe calme a peace
reate Mars could not greater tempest fayne
hen the lowd windes, spurring on the Mayne
or angrie Juno labour'd to destroy
he hated reliques of confounded Troy
is bold ENEAS on like billows tost
n a tall Shipp, and all his Countreys lost
issolves with feare, and both his hands upheld
roclaymes them happie, whome the Greeks had queld
n honourable fight, our Heroe sett
a small Shallopp, Fortune in his debt
re neare a hope of Crowne, and Scepters, more
hen ever Pryam, when hee flourish'd, were
is loynes yet full of yongest Princes, all
is glorie in the Budd, letts nothing fall
hat argues feare: If any thought annoys
he gallant youth, tis Loves untasted ioyes
nd deare remembrance of that fatall glance
or which hee lately pawn'd his hearte in ffrance
where hee had seene a brighter Nymph then shee
That sprung out of his present foe, the Sea;
That noble ardour, more then mortall fire
The conquer'd ocean could not make expire
Nor angrie Thetis rayse her waves above
The heroigh Prince his Courage or his Love
Twas Indignation, not feare hee felt
The Prince Could perrish, where that Image dwelt
Ah Love forbidd the noblest of thy trayne
Should not survive, to let her knowe his paine
Who nor his perrill minding nor his flame
H'entertain'd wth some less serious game
Among the bright Nymphs of the Gallick Court
All highlie borne, obsequious to her sport
They roses seeme, wch in their earlie pride
But halfe reveale, and halfe their beauties hide
When the glad morning with her Beames doth bestowe
Upon the smiling leaves, and guild them soe;

Like Bright Aurora, whose refulgent rays
Foretells the fervour of ensuing day
And warns the Shepheard with his flocks retreat
To leafie shadowes, from the threatned heate
From Cupids string of many shafts that fledd
Wing'd with those plumes, which noble fame had shedd
As through the wondring world, shee flew, and told
Of his adventures, haughtie, brave, and bold
Some had alreadie touch't the royall Mayde
But Loves first Summons seldome are obey'd
Light was the wound, the Prince his face unknowne
She might not, would not yet reveale her owne
His glorious name had soe possest her eares
That with delight, those Antique tayles she heares
Of Jason Theseus, and such worthies old
As with his Storie best resemblance hold
And now she viewes, as on the wall it hung
What old Musæus soe divinely sung
Which Art with Love, and Life did soe inspire
That she discernes, and favours yt desire
Which there provokes th'adventurous youth to swimm
And in Leanders danger pitties him
Whose not now Love alone but fortune seekes
To frame his storie, like yt Amarous Greekes
For from the sterne of some good Shipp appeares
A friendly light, which moderates their feares
New courage from reviving hope they take
And clymbing ore the waves yt taper make
On which the hope of all their life depends
As his on that faire Heroes hand depends
The Shipp att Anchor like a fixed rocke
Breakes the proud Billows, which her large side knocke
Whose rage restrayn'd foaming higher swells
And from her Port, the wearie Barge repells
Threatninge to make her (forced out againe)
Repeate the dangers of the troubled Mayne
Twice was the Cable hurl'd in vaine, the fates
Would not bee moved for our Sister States
For England is the third successfull throne
And then the Genius of that Land they knowe
Whose Prince must bee (as their owne books devise)
Lord of the Ocean, where now his danger lyes.

Well sung the Roman bard all humane things
Of dearest value hang on slender strings
Oh see the then sole hope, and in designe
Of heaven, our Joy's supported by a lyne
Which for that instant was heavens care above
The Chayne that's fixed to the throane of Jove
On which the ffabrick of our World depends
One lynke dissolved, the whole Creation ends. /

Of his Ma:ties receivinge the Newes of the Duke of Buck: Deathe

e earnest with thy God, can not now care
r sense of danger interrupt thy prayre
e sacred Wrastler till a blessing given
uitts not his hold, but halting conquers heaven
or was the streame of thy devotion stopt
hen from the bodie, such a Limbe was lopt
e to thy present state, was noe lesse mayme
hough thy wise choyce hath since repayr'd the same
old Homer durst not soe greate Vertue fayne
n his best patterne for Patroclus slayne
vith such amazement as weake Mothers use
nd frantique gestures, hee receives the newes
et fell his darling by the impartiall chance
Of warr, imposed by royall Hectors Lance
hine in full peace, and by a vulgar hand
orne from thy bosome, left his high Command
he famous Painter could allowe noe place
or private sorrowe in a Princes face
et that his peace might not exceede beleife
e cast a Veyle on Agamemnons greife
was want of such a President as this
Made the old heathen frame their Gods amiss
heir Phebus should not act a fonder parte
for the fayre Boy, then hee did for his hearte
Nor blame for Hyacinthus fate his owne
that kept him from wish'd deathe, hadst thou byn knowne

Yet hee which weighs wth thine Good Davids deeds
Shall finde his passion, not his Love exceeds
Hee curs'd the mountaines, where his brave freind dy'd
Yet lett false Ziba with his heire devide
Where thy immortall Love to thy blest freind
Like that of heaven upon their seede descend
Such huge extreames inhabit thy greate minde
Godlike unmov'd, and yet like woman kinde
Which of the ancient Poets had not brought
Our Charles his pedigree from heaven, and taught
How some bright Dame compress'd by mighty Iove
Produc'd this mixt divinitie, and Love.

Upon his Maties: repayringe of Paules Church

That Shipwrack't vessell which the Apostle bore
Scarce suffer'd more upon Miletas shore
Then did his temple in the sea of time
Our Nations glorie, and our Nations crime
When the first Monarch of this happie Isle
Mov'd with the ruyne of soe brave a pile
This worke of cost, and pietie begunn
To bee accomplish'd by this glorious Sunn
Whoe all that came within the ample thought
Of his wise Syre hath to perfection brought
Hee like Amphion makes those Quarries leape
Into fayre figures from a confused heape
For in his Art of Regiment is found
A Power like that of harmonie in sound
Those Antique Minstrells sure were Charles-like Kings
Cities their Lutes, and Subiects hearts the strings
On which, with soe divine a hand they strooke
Consent of motion from their breathe they tooke
Soe all our minds with his conspire to grace
The Gentiles greate Apostle, and deface

Those

Those State obscuring shadds, that like a chayne
Seeme to confine, and fetter him againe
Which the glad Saint shakes of, att his comande
As once the Viper from his sacred hand
Soe ioyes the aged Oake, when he divides
The creeping Ivy from his iniur'd side
Ambition rather would affecte the fame
Of some new Structure to have borne his name
Twoe distant vertues in one Act wee finde,
The modestie and greatnes of his minde
Which not content to bee above the rage
And iniurie of all Impairing Age
In its owne worth secure doth higher clymbe
And things halfe swallowed from the iawes of time
Reduce, an earnest of his grand designe
To frame noe new church, but the old refyne
Which Spouse-like may with comely grace comand
More then by force of Argument or hand
For doubtfull reason, few cann apprehend
And Warr brings ruyne, where it should amend
But beautie with a bloodless conquest finds
A welcome Soveraignty in rudest minds
Not ought, which Shebaes wandring Queene beheld
Among the works of Solomon excelld
His Ships and buildings, Emblemes of a heart
Large both in magnanimitie, and Art
While the propitious Heavens this worke attend
Long wanted showers they have forgott to send
As if they meant to make it understood
Of more Importance then our vitall food
The Sunn which riseth to salute the Quire
Alreadie finish'd, setting shall admire

How private bountie could soe farr extend.
The King builds all, But Charles the Westerne End.
Soe proud a ffabricke to devotion given
Att once it threatneth, and obligeth Heaven
Laomedon that had the Gods in pay
Neptune with him that rules the sacred Day
Could not such Structure rayse, Troy walld soe high
The Atrides might as soone have forc'd the Skye
Glad though amazed are our neighbour Kings
To see such power imployed in peacefull things
They list not urge it, to the dreadfull ffeild
The taske is easier to destroy then build.

To the QUEENE occasioned upon sight of her Ma:tiis Picture./

Well fare the hand, which to our humble sight
Presents that Beautie, which the dazeling light
Of royall Splendo: hides from weaker eyes
And all accesse (save by this Art) denyes
Heere wee have only courage to behold
This Beame of glory, heere wee dare unfold
In numbers thus the wonders wee conceive
The gracious Image seeming to give leave
Propitious stands vouchsafing to be seene
And by our Muse saluted.
Mightie QUEENE
In whome the extreams of power, and beautie move
The Queene of Brittain, and the Queene of Love
As the bright Sunn (to which wee owe noe sight
Of equall glorie to his beautious light
Is wisely plac't in soe sublyme a Seate
T'extend his light, and moderate his heate
Soe happie 'tis you move in such a Sphaere
As yo:r high Ma:tie with awfull feare
In humane breasts might qualifie that fire
Which kindled by those eyes had flamed higher
Then when the scorched world like hazard runn
By the approach of the ill guided Sunn
Noe other Nimphs have titles to mens hearts
But as their meanes larger hope imparts
Yo:r beautie more the fondest Lover move
With admiration then his private Love
With admiration, for a pitch soe high
Save sacred Charles his; never Love durst fly
Heaven that preferd a Scepter to yo:r hand
Favour'd our Freedome more then yo:r command
Beautie had crownd you, and you must have been
The whole worlds Mistress: other then a QUEENE

All had byn rivalls, and you might have spar'd
And kild, or tyranniz'd without a guard
Noe power atcheiv'd either by Armes or Birth
Equalls Loves Empire both in Heaven and Earth
Such eyes as yo:rs on Jove himselfe had throwne
As bright, and fierce a lightning as his owne
Witnes our Jove, prevented by their flame
In his swift passage to the Hesperian DAME
When like a Lyon finding in his way
To some intended spoyle, a fairer prey
The royall youth pursuing the report
Of Beautie, found it in the Gallick Court
There publique care, with private passion fought
A doubtfull combate in his noble thought
Should hee confesse his Greatnes, and his Love
And the free fayth of yo:r owne Brother prove
With his Achates breaking through the Clowde
Of that disguise, which did their graces shrowde
And mixing with those Gallants att the Ball
Dance with the Ladie, and outshine them all
Or in his Journey over the mountaines ride
Soe when the fayre LEUCOTHOE he espi'd
To checke his steeds impatient Phebus earn'd
But all the world was in his Coarse concern'd
What may hereafter her Meridian doe
Whose Dawninge Beautie, warm'd his bosome soe
Not soe divine a fflame, since deathles Gods
fforbore to visite the defil'd abodes
Of men, in any mortall breast did burne
Nor shall till Pietie, and they returne./

Of Love!

[A]nger in hastie words, or blowes
[It]selfe dischargeth on our ffoes
[A]nd Sorrowe too findes some releife
[I]n teares which wayte upon our greife
Soe every passion but fond Love
Unto its owne redresse doth move
But that alone the wretch inclines
To what prevents his owne designes
Makes him lament, and sigh, and weepe
Disorder'd, tremble, fawne, and creepe
Postures that render him despis'd
where hee endeavours to bee priz'd.
For women borne to bee contrould
Stoope to the forward, and the bold
Affecte the haughtie, and the proud
The gay, the frollicke, and the loud
Whoe first the generous Steede opprest
Not kneeling did salute the Beast
But with high courage, life, and force
Approaching tam'd the unruly horse
And wisely wee, the wiser East
Pittie supposing them opprest
With Tyrants force, whose Lawe is Will
By which they governe spoyle, and kill
Each Nymph but moderately fayre
Comands with noe less rigour heere
Should some Brave Turke, who walkes among
His twentie Lasses bright and Young
And beckons to the willing Dame
Prefer'd to quench his present flame
Behold as many Gallants heere
With modest guise, and silent feare
All to one female Idoll bend
While her high pride doth scarce descend
To marke their follies hee would sweare
That these her Guard of Eunuches were

And that a more Maiestique Queene
Or humbler Slaves hee had not seene
All this with Indignation spake
In vaine I strugl'd with the yoake
Of mightie Love, that conquering looke
When next beheld, like lightning strooke
My blasted Soule, and made mee bow
Lower then those I pittyed now.
Soe the tall Stagg upon the brincke
Of some smooth streame about to drincke
Surveying there his armed head,
With shame remembers that he fledd.
The scorned dogges, resolve to try
The combate next, but if theire cry
Invades againe his trembling eare
Hee straight resumes his wonted feare
Leaves the untasted spring behinde
And wing'd with feare, outflyes the winde.

Upon the Mutable Faire

Heere Cælia for thy sake I part
With all that grew soe neere my hearte
The passion which I had for thee
The fayth, the Love, the Constancie
And that I may successfull proove
Transforme my selfe to what you love
ffoole that I was, soe much to prize
Those simple Vertues you despise
ffoole that with such dull arrowes strove
Or hop'd to reach a flyinge Dove
ffor you that are in motion still
Decline our force, and mocke our skill
Who like Don Quixot does advance
Against a windmill, our vaine Launce
Now will I wander through the ayre
Mount, make a stoope, at every fayre
And with a fancie unconfin'd
(As lawles as the Sea, or wind)

rsue you, wheresoere you fly
with your various thoughts comply
e formall starrs doe travell soe
wee their names, and courses knowe
d hee that on their changes lookes
ould thinke them govern'd by our bookes
ut never were the Clowds reduc'd
any Art, the motions us'd
y those free vapours, are soe light
ee frequent, that the conquer'd sight
espaires to finde the rule, which guide
hose guilded shadows as they slyde
nd therefore of the spatious ayre
ves royall consort had the care
nd by that power did once escape
eclyning bold Ixions rape
he with her owne resemblance grac'd
shyning Cloud which hee embrac'd
uch was that Image, soe it smil'd
ith seeming kindnes, which beguil'd
o:r Thirsis lately, whome he thought
ee had his fleeting Cælia caught
was shap'd like her, but for the fayre
ee fil'd his armes with yeilding ayre
ffate for which hee greives the loss
Because the Gods had like successe
For in their storie, one wee see
Pursues a Nymph, and takes a tree
second with a Lovers hast
Soone overtakes, whome hee had chac'd
But shee that did a Virgin seeme
Possest, appeares a wandring streame
For his supposed Love a third
ayes greedie hold, upon a Bird
nd stands amaz'd to finde his deare
wylde Inhabitant of the ayre
e theis old tales such Nymphs as you
ive creditt, and still make them new
he Amorous now, like wonders finde
n the swift changes of yo:r minde.

But Cælia if you apprehend
The Muse of yo.r incensed ffreind
Nor would that hee record yo.r blame
And make it live; repeate the same
Againe deceive him, and againe
And then hee sweares, hee'l not complaine.
ffor still to bee deluded soe
Is all the pleasure Lovers knowe
Whoe like good ffaulkners take delight
Not in the Quarry, but the flight./

Songe

While I listen to thy voice
Cloris I feele my life decay
that powerfull noyse
Calls my fleeting Soule away
Oh suppresse that Magicke sounde
Which destroys without a wound:

Peace Cloris peace, or singing dye
That together you and I
To heaven may goe
ffor all wee knowe
Of what the blessed doe above
Is that they sing, and that they Love./

See 8 leaves forward

To Phillis

illis why should wee delay
easure shorter then the day
ld wee, which wee never cann
etche our Lives beyond their spann
autie like a shadowe flyes
d our Youth before us dyes
would wee make beautie stay
e hath wings, and will away
ve hath swifter wings then time
ange in Love to heaven doth clime
ds that never change their State
arie oft their Love and Hate:
illis to this breathe wee owe
the Love betwixt us now
t not you, and I enquire
hat hath byn our hearts desire
ave it to the honoured Crew
hat hereafter wee must doe
r the ioys wee now may prove
ke advice of present Love./

To Flavia

s not yo: Beautie cann engage
My wary Hearte
e Sunn in all his pride and rage
Hath not that Art
d yet hee shines as bright as you
brightnes could our Soules subdue.

s not the pretty things you say
Or that you write
hich can make Thirsis hearte your pray
For that delight
e graces of a well taught minde
Some of our owne Sex wee finde./

Noe Flavia 'tis not Love I feare
Loves surest darts
Those which soe seldome fayle him, are
Headed with Hearts
Their very shadowes make us yeild
Dissemble well, and take the feild./

To the King on his Navy

Where ere thy Navie spreads her Canvas wings
Homage to thee, and peace to all she brings
The French, and Spaniard, when thy flaggs appeare
Forgett their hatred, and consent to feare:
Soe Jove from Ida did both hosts survey,
And when hee pleas'd to thunder, part the fray
Shipps heeretofore in Seas like Fishes sped.
The mightiest still upon the smallest fedd.
Thou on the deepe imposest stricter Lawes
And by that Justice hath removed the cause
Of those rude tempests, which for rapine sent
Too oft (alas) involv'd the Innocent
Now shall thy Ocean as thy Thames bee free
From both those fates of Stormes, and Pyracie
But wee most happie, whoe cann feare noe force
But winged Troopes, or Pegasean horse
Tis not soe hard for greedie foes to spoyle
Another Nation, as to touch our Soyle
Should Natures selfe invade the World againe
And o're the Center spread the Liquid Mayne
Thy power were safe, and her destructive hand
Should but inlarge the bounds of thy Command
Thy dreadfull Fleete would style thee Lord of all
And ride in triumph o're the drowned Ball
Those Towers of Oake o're fertile plains must goe
And visitt mountains, where they once did growe
The worlds restorer could not once indure
That finisht Babell should those men secure

hose pride desyr'd that Fabricke to have stood
ove the reach of any Second Flood
ie to his chosen more indulgent, Hee
nor trust such power, wth Sommers pittie./

Of the takinge of Salley./

Of Jason Theseus, and those worthies old
ight seeme the Tales Antiquitie hath told
uch Beasts and Monsters as their force opprest
ome places only, and some times infest
alley that scorn'd all power, and lawes of men
oods with their Owners hurrying to their Den
nd future Ages threatning with a rude
nd savadge Race successively renew'de
heir King despising with rebellious pride
nd Foes profest to all the world beside
his Pest of Mankinde gives our Heroe fame
nd through the obliged world dilates his name:
he Prophett once to cruell Agag sayd
thy fierce sword hath Mothers Childles made
oe shall the sword make thine, and with that word
ee hew'd the Prince in peeces, with his sword
st Charles like measure hath return'd to these
hose Pagan hands hath stayn'd the bloodie Seas
ith Shipps they made the spoyled Merchant mourne
ith Shipps their Cittie, and themselves are torne
ne Squadron of our winged Castles sent
rethrew their forte, and all their Navie rent
or not content the dangers to increase
nd acte the parte of Tempests in the Seas
ke hungry Wolves these Pyrats from our Shoare
hole flocks of Sheepe, and ravish't cattle bore
afely they did on other Nations prey
oles to provoke the Soveraigne of the Sea
ad Cacus so whome like ill fate perswades
he heard of faire Alcmenas Seede invades
hoe for revenge, and mortalls gladd releife
ack'd the darke Cave, and crush'd the horrid theife

Moroccoes Monarch wondring att this fact
Save that his presence his affaires d'bart
Had come in person to have seene, and knowne
The injur'd worlds revenger, and his owne
Hither hee sends the choise among his Peers
whoe in his Barque well chosen Presents bears
To the renowned for Pietie, and Powre
Poore Captives manumiz'd and matchles horse. /

The Apologie of Somnus for not approaching the Ladie whoe can doe any thing but sleepe when she pleaseth

My charge it is, those breaches to repayre
Which Nature takes from Sorrow, toyle, and care
Rest to the Limbs, and quiett I confer
On troubled minds, but nought can add to her
Whome Heaven, and her transcendent thoughts have plac'd
Above those Ills which wretched Mortalls tast
Bright as the deathles Gods, and happie soe
From (all that may infringe) delight is free
Love att her royall Foote his Quivers layes
And not his mother with more hast obeys
Such reall pleasures, such true joys surround
What dreams can I present to recompence
Should (with) lightning fill her awfull hand
And make the Clouds seeme all att her command
Or place her in Olympus topp, a guest
Among the Immortalls whoe with Nectar feast
That power would seeme, that entertainment sport
Of the true splendour of her present Court
Where all the joys, and all the glories are
Of Three greate Kingdomes secur'd from the care
That of fumes, and humid vapours made
Ascending doe the state of Sleepe invade
Nor Clouds in soe serene a Mansion finde
To overcast her evershining mind
Which holds resemblance with those spotles skyes
Where flowing Nilus want of rayne supplies

at cristall heaven, where Phebus never shrouds
is golden beames, nor wrapps his face in clouds
ut what soe hard which numbers cannot force
oe stoopes the Moone, and rivers change their course
he bold Maeonian made mee dare to steepe
ves dreadfull temples in the dew of sleepe
nd since the Muses doe invoake my power
shall noe more decline that sacred bower
ut gently taming those victorious eyes
here Gloriana their greate M^rs lyes
harme all her senses, till the ioyfull sunn
ithout a Rivall halfe his course hath runn
whoe while my hand, that fairer light confines
May boast himselfe the brightest thing that shines./

The Countrey to my Ladie of Carlisle./

Madam

Of all the sacred Muse inspir'd
Orpheus alone could with the Woods comply
Their rude Inhabitants his Song admir'd
And Nature selfe, in those that could not lye
Your beautie next our Solitude invades
And warmes us shining through our thickest shades
Nor ought the tribute which the wondring Court
Payes yor faire eyes, prevayle with you to scorne
The Answer, and consent to that report
Which Echoe-like the Countrey doth returne
Mirrors are taught to flatter, but our Springs
Present the impartiall Images of things
A rurall Iudge, dispos'd of beauties prize
A simple Shepheard was prefer'd to Jove
Downe to the Mountaines from the partiall skyes
Come Juno, Pallas, and the Queene of Love
To pleade for that which was soe iustly given
To the Bright Carlisle of the Court of Heaven

Carlisle a Name which all the Woods are taught
Lowd as his Amarillis to resound
Carlisle a Name, which on the Barke is wrought
Of every tree thats thought worthy of the Wound
From Phebus rage, our shadowes, and our Streames
May guard us better, then from Carlisle Beames. /

Madam

As in some Clymes the warmer Sunn
Makes it full Summer, ere our Springs begunn
And with ripe fruite the bending Boughes can load
Before our Violetts dare looke abroad
Soe measure not by any common use
The early Love yo:r brighter eyes produce
When lately yo:r faire hand, (in womans weede)
Wrapt my glad head I wisht mee so indeede
That hastie time might never make mee growe
Out of those favours you afford mee now
That I might ever such Indulgence finde
And you not blush, or thinke yo:r selfe too kinde
Who now I feare while I these joyes expresse
Beginn to thinke how you may make them lesse
The sounde of Love makes yo:r soft hearte afrayd
And guard it selfe, though but a childe invade
And innocently att yo:r white breast throwe
A dart as white, a Ball of new falne Snowe. /

R Waller. /

The Countesse of Carlisle in Mourninge./

When from blacke Clouds, noe parte of Skye is cleare
But Just soe much as letts the Sunn appeare
Heaven then would seeme thy Image, and reflect
Those sable Vestments, and that bright aspect
A sparke of Vertue by the deepest shade
Of sadd adversitie is fayrer made
Nor less advantage doth thy Beautie gett
A Venus rising from a Sea of Jett
Such was the appearance of new formed light
While yett it strugled with Eternall night
Then mourne noe more, least thou admitt increase
Of glorie, by thy noble Lords decease
Wee finde not that the laughter-loving Dame
Mourn'd for Anchises, 'twas enough shee came
To grace the Mortall, with her deathles Bed
And that his living eyes such beautie fedd
Had shee byn there, untimely ioy through all
Mens hearts diffused, had marr'd the ffunerall
Those eyes were made to banish greife, aswell
Bright Phebus might affecte in shades to dwell
As they to putt on sorrowe, nothing stands
But power to greive exempt from thy commands
If thou lament, thou must doe soe alone
Greife in thy presence cann lay hold of none
Yet still persist the memorie to love
Of that greate Mercurie of our mightie Jove
Who by the power of his inchanting tounge
Swords from the hands of threatning Monarchs wrung
Warr hee prevented, or soone made it cease
Instructing Princes in the Arts of Peace
Such as made Shebaes curious Queene resort
To the large hearted Hebrews famous Court
Had Homer satt among his wondring Guests
Hee might have learn'd att those stupendious ffeasts

With greater Bountie, and more sacred State
The Banquetts of the Gods to celebrate
But oh what Elocution might hee use
What potent charmes, that could soe soone infuse
His absent Masters Love into the hearte
Of Henrietta forcing her to parte
From her lov'd Brother Countrey and the Sunn
And like Camilla, ore the waves to runn
Into his Armes, while the Parisian Dames
Mourne for their ravisht glorie att her flames
Noe less amazed then the amazed starrs
When the bold Charmer of Thessalia Warrs
With Heaven it selfe, and numbers does ~~[illegible]~~ repeate
Which call descending Cynthia from her Seate./

Att Penshurst

While in this Parke I sing, the listning Deere
Attend my passion, and forgett to feare
When to the Beeches I report my flame
They Bow their heads as if they felt the same
To Gods appealing, when I reach their Bowers
With loud complaints, they answer mee in showers
To thee, a wilde and cruell Soule is given
More deafe then trees, and prowder then the heavens
Loves foe profest, why dost thou falsly faine
Thy selfe a Sidney, from which noble strayne
Hee sprung, that could soe farr exalt the name
Of Love, and warme our Nation with his flame
That all wee cann of Love our high desire
Seems but the smoake of Amorous Sidneys fire
Nor call her Mother, whoe soe well does prove
One Breast may hold bote chastitie, and Love
Never cann Shee that soe exceeds the Spring
In Ioy, and bountie, bee supposd to bring

But thee destructive, to noe eminent Rocke
Wee owe this fierce unkindnes, but the rocke
That cloven rocke produc'd thee, by whose side
Nature to recompence the fatall pride
Of such sterne beautie, plac'd those healing springs
Which not more helpe, then that destruction brings
Thy hearte noe ruder then that rugged stone
I might with Orpheus with my numerous moane
Melt to compassion, now my traytorous song
With thee conspires to doe the Singer wrong
While thus I suffer not my selfe to loose
The memorie of what augments my woes
But with my owne breath still foment the fire
Which flames as high, as flame can aspire
This last complaint, th'indulgent eares did peirce
Of iust Apollo President of Verse
Highly concern'd, that the Muse should bring
Damadge to one, whome hee had taught to sing
Thus hee advis'd mee; On yon aged Tree
Hang up thy Lute, and hye thee to the Sea
That there with wonders, thy diverted minde
Some truce at least may with affliction finde
Ah cruell Nymph, from whome her humble Swaine
Flyes for releife unto the raging Mayne
And from the winds, and tempests doth expect
A milder fate, then from her cold neglect
Yet there heele pray, that she unkind may prove
Blest in her choyce, and vow this endles Love
Springs from noe hope of what hee can confer
But from those guifts, wch Heaven has heap'd on her. /

A La: Malade

Ah lovely Amorett the care
Of all that knowe whats good or fayre
Is heaven become our Rivall too
Had the rich guifts confer'd on you
Soe amply thence the common end
Of giving Lovers to pretend.
Hence to this pining Sicknes (meant
To wearie thee to a consent
Of leaving us) noe power is given
Thy beauties to impaire from heaven
Sollicites thee with such a care
As roses from the stalks wee tare
When wee would still preserve them new
And fresh as on the Bush they grew
With such a grace you entertaine
And looke with such contempt on paine
That languishing you conquer more
And wound us deeper then before
The lightnings which in storms appeare
Scorch more, then when the Skies are cleare
And as pale Sicknes does invade
Your frayler parte the breaches made
In that faire lodging, still more cleare
Make the bright guest yor. Soule appeare
Soe Nymphs ore pathles Mountains borne
Their Light robes by the brambles torne
From their faire Limbs, exposing new
And unknowne beauties to the view
Of following Gods increase their flame
And haste to catch the flying Game./

For the Drinckinge of Healths

All Bruits, and Vegitalls that cannott thincke
oe farr as drought, and Nature needs, drincke
more Indulgent Mistress guides our sprights
eason that dares beyond our appetites
hee would our care, aswell as thirst redresse
nd with Divinitie rewards excesse
esorted Ariadne thus supplyd
id perjurd Theseus crueltie deryde
Bacchus imbrac'd from her exalted thought
Banish'd the man, her passion, and his faute
Bacchus and Phebus are by Love allyd
And each by others timely heate supplyd
All that the grapes owe to his ripening fires
Is paid in numbers, which their Iuyce inspires
Wine fills the Veyns, and healths are understood
To give our freinds a title to our blood
Who naming mee doth warme his courage soe
Shows for my sake, what his bold hand would doe./

Songe

Goe lovely rose
Tell her that wasts her time and mee
That now shee knowes
When I resemble her to thee
How sweete, and fayre shee seems to bee

Tell her that's young
And shuns to have her graces spyde
That hadst thou sprung
In deserts where noe men abyde
Thou must have uncomended dyde.

Small is the worth
Of beautie from the light retyr'd.
Bid her come forth
Suffer herselfe to bee desir'd.
And not blush soe to bee admir'd.

Then dye, that shee
The common fate of all things rare
May reade in thee
How small a parte of time they share
That are soe wondrous sweete, and fayre./

On the Discoverie of a Ladies paintinge

Pigmalions fate reverst is mine
His marble love tooke flesh, and blood.
All that I worshipt as divine
That beautie now 'tis understood.
Appeares noe more to have of life
Then that whereof hee fram'd his wife

As women yet who apprehend.
Some sodaine cause of causeles feare
Although that seeming cause take end.
And they behold noe danger neere
A shaking through their limbs they finde
Like leaves saluted by the winde

Soe though the beautie doe appeare
Noe beautie which amaz'd mee soe
Yet from my breast I cannott teare
The passion which from thence did growe
Nor yet out of my phansie raze
The print of that supposed face

A reall beautie (though too neere)
The fond Narcissus did admire
I doate on that which is not there
The signe of beautie feeds my fire
Noe mortall flame was ere soe cruell
As this, which thus survives the fewell./

Of her Chamber

hey taste of deathe, that doe att Heaven arrive
But wee the Paradise approach alive
nstead of Death the dart of Love, does strike
nd renders all within theis walls alike
he high in titles, and the Sherpheard heere
forgetts his greatnes, and forgets his feare
ll stand amazd, and gazing on the fayre
oose thought of what themselves, or others are
mbition loose, and have noe other scope
ave Carlisles favour to imploy their hope
The Thracian could (though all those tales were true
The bold Greeke tell) noe greater wonders doe
Before his feete soe Sheepe, and Lyons lay
ffearles and wrathles, while they heard them play
The Gay, the wise the Gallant, and the Grave
Subdude alike all but one passion Have
Noe worthy minde but findes in her there is
Something proportiond to the rule of his
While shee with cheerefull but impartiall Grace
(Borne for noe one, but to delight the race
Of men) like Phebus soe devides her light
And warms vs that she stoopes not from her height./

Of Lovinge att the first Sight./

Noe caringe to observe the winde
Or the new Sea explore
Snatcht from my selfe, how farr behinde
Alreadie I behold the Shore
May not a thousand dangers sleepe
In the smooth bosome of this deepe:
Noe: tis soe rockles, and soe cleere
That the rich bottome does appeare
Pav'd all with pretious things, not torne
ffrom shipwrackt Vessells, but there borne
Sweetnes, truth, and every grace
Which time, and vse are wont to teach

The Eye may in a moment reach
And reade distinctly in her face
Some other Nimphs with colours faynt
And pensill slowe may Cupid paynt
And a weake heart in time destroy
Shee has a Stamp, and prints the Boy
Cann with a single looke inflame
The coldest breast, the rudest tame./

Of the Queene

The Larke that shuns on loftie boughs to build
Her humble nest, lyes silent in the field
But if the promise of a cloudles day
(Aurora smiling) bids her rise, and play
Then straight shee showes twas not for want of Voyce
Or power to clymbe, shee made soe low a choyce
Singing shee mounts, her ayrie wings are stretcht
Towards heaven, as if from heav'n her note she fetcht
Soe wee retyring from the busie throng
Use to restrayne th'ambition of our Song
But since the light, which now informs our age
Breaks from the Court, indulgent to her rage
Thither my Muse like bold Prometheus flyes
To light her torch att Gloriana's Eyes
Those Soveraigne beams, which heale the wounded Soule
And all our cares, but once behold controwle
There the poore Lover, that has long endur'd
Some proud Nymphs scorne, of his fond passion cur'd
Fares like the Man, whoe first upon the grounde
A glowe worme spyde, supposing hee had found
A moving dyamond, a breathing stone
(For life that had, and like those Jewells shone)
Hee held that deare, till by the springing day
Inform'd hee threw the worthles worme away
Shee saves the Lover, as wee Gangrines stay
By cutting hope, like a lost limbe away:

his makes her bleeding Patients to accuse
High Heaven, and these expostulations use
ould Nature then noe private woman grace
Whome wee might dare to love) wth. such a face
Such a Complexion, and soe radiant Eyes
Such lovely motion, and such sharpe replyes
Beyond our reach, and yet within our sight
What envious power has plac'd this glorious light

Thus in a starrie night fond children cry
For the rich spangles that adorne the Skye
Which though they shine for ever fixed there
With light, and influence releive vs heere
All her afflictions are to one inclinde
Her bountie and compassion to mankinde
To whome while shee soe farr extends her grace
Shee makes but good the promise of her face
For mercie has (could mercies selfe bee seene)
Noe sweeter looke, then this propitious Queene
Such guard and comfort the distressed finde
From her large power, and her larger minde
That whome ill fate would ruyne, it preferrs
For all the miserable are made hers
Soe the fayre tree, whereon the Eagle builds
Poore sheepe from tempest, and their Shepheards sheilds
The royall Bird possesses all the Boughs
But shade and shelter to the flocke allows.

Joy of our Age, and safetie of the next
For which soe oft thy fertile wombe is vext
Nobly contented for the publique good
To waste thy spiritts and diffuse thy blood
What vast hopes may these Islands entertaine
Where Monarchs thus descended are to raigne
Led by Comanders of soe faire a Lyne
Our Seas noe longer shall our power confyne

A brave Romance whoe would exactly frame
First brings his Knight, from some immortall Dame
And then a weapon, and a flaming sheild
Bright as his Mothers eyes; Hee makes him weild

None might the mother of Achilles bee
But the faire pearle, and glorie of the Sea
The man to whome greate Mars gives such fame
From the high bed of Heavenly Venus came
And our next Charles (whome all the starrs designe
Like wonders to accomplish) springs from thine./

Of a Ladie whoe writt in prayse of Myra.

While shee pretends to make the graces knowne
Of matchles Myra, she reveals her owne
And when shee would anothers prayse endite
Is by her glass instructed how to write./

Of one married to an old Man

Since thou wouldst needs, bewitch'd with some ill charms
Bee buried in those monumentall Armes
All wee can wish is, may that Earth lye light
Upon thy tender Limbs, and soe good night./

Puerperium.

You Gods that have the power
To trouble and compose
All that's beneath yor. Bower
Calme, Silence on the Seas, on earth impose.

Faire Venus in thy soft armes
The God of rage confine
For thy whispers are the charmes
Which only can divert his fierce designe.

What though hee frowne, and to tumult doe inclyne
Thou the flame
Kindled in his breast canst tame
With that snowe which unmelted lyes on thine./

Greate Goddess give this thy sacred Island rest
Make Heaven smile
That noe storme disturbe us while
Thy cheife care our Halcion builds her nest.
Greate Gloriana ffaire Gloriana
Bright as high Heaven is, and fertile as earth,
Whose beautie releives us
Whose royall bed gives us
Both glorie and Peace
Our present Joy, our hopes increase.

Songe

hile I listen to thy Voice
loris I feele my life decay
That powerfull noyse
ills my fleeting Sowle away
h suppress that Magicke sound
which destroys without a Wound

s
eace Chloris peace, or singing dye
That togeather you and I
To heaven may goe
ffor all wee knowe
Of what the blessed doe above
Is that they sing, and that they Love.

See 8 Leaves before

Songe

Stay Phebus stay
The world to which you fly soe fast
Conveying Day
From us to them can pay yo:r hast
With noe such obiects, nor salute yo:r rise
With noe such wonders as De Mornays Eyes:

Well does this prove
The error of those antique Bookes
Which made you move
About the world, her charminge Lookes
Would fix yo:r beames, and make it ever Day
Did not the rowling earth snatch her away:/

The Selfe Banished

It is not that I love you less
Then when before your feete I lay
But to prevent the sad increase
Of hopeles Love, I keepe away)

In vaine (alas) for every thing
Which I have knowne belong to you
Your forme does to my fancie bring
And make my old wounds bleede anew:

Whome the Spring, from the new Sunne
Already has a ffeavour gott
Too late beginns those shafts to shunn
Which Phebus through his veyns has shott:

To late hee would the paine asswage
And to thicke shadowes does retire
About with him hee beares the rage
And in his tainted blood the fire

But vow'd I have, and never must
Yo:r banish'd servant trouble you
ffor if I breake you may mistrust
The vow I made to love you too. /

Thirsis. Galatea. /

As lately I on silver Thames did ride
Sad Galatea on the banke I spyde
Such was her looke, as sorrow taught to shine
And thus she grac'd mee with a voyce divine.

G: You that can tune yo:r sounding strings soe well
Of Ladies beauties, and of Love to tell
Once change yo:r noate, and let yo:r Lute report
The iustest greife, that ever touch'd the Court

Fayre Nymphes I have in yo:r delights noe share
Nor ought to bee concerned in yo:r care
Yet would I sing if I yo:r sorrows knew
And to my ayde invoake noe Muse but you

G: Heare then and lett yo:r song augment our greife
Which is soe greate, as not to wish releife
Shee that had all which Nature gives, or Chance
Whome ffortune ioyn'd with vertue to advance
To all the Ioys this Island could afforde
The greatest Mistress, and the kindest Lorde
Who with the royall mixt her noble blood
And in high grace wth Gloriana stood
Her bountie, sweetnes, beautie, goodnes such
That none ere thought her happines too much

Soe well inclyn'd her favours to confer
And kinde to all as Heaven had byn to her
The Virgins parte, the Mother and the Wife
Soe well she acted in this spann of life
That though few yeares (too few alas) she told.
Shee seem'd in all things, but in beautie, old.
As unripe fruite, whose verdant stalke doth cleave
Close to the tree, which greives noe less to leave
The smiling pendant which adornes her soe
And untill Autumne on the bough should growe
Soe seem'd her youthfull soule not easly forc'd
Or from soe faire soe sweete a seate divorc'd
Her Fate at once did hastie seeme, and slowe
All once too cruell, and unwilling too.

Ch: Under how hard a Lawe are mortalls borne
Whome now wee envie, wee anon must mourne
What Heaven setts highest, and seemes most to prize
Is soone removed from our wondring eyes
But since the Sisters did soe soone untwine
Soe faire a thread Ile strive to reare the Lyne
Vouchsafe (sad Nymphe) to lett mee knowe the Dame
And to the Muses Ile commend her name
Make the wide Countrey Eccho to yo: moane
The listning trees, and savadge mountains groane
What rock's not moved when the death is sung
Of one soe good, soe lovely, and soe young

Sal: 'Twas Hamilton whome (I had nam'd before
But naming her greife lets mee say noe more.

The Battaile of the Summer Islands

Canto :1:

What fruite they have and how Heaven smiles
Upon those late discovered Isles

Ayde mee Bellona while the dreadfull fight
Betwixt twoe Nations, and a Whale I write
Seas stayn'd with goare I sing, adventrous toyle
And how these Monsters did disarme an Isle
Bermudas wall'd with rocks who does not knowe
That happie Island where huge Lemmons growe
And Orrange trees which golden fruite doe beare
Th' Hesperian garden boasts of none soe faire
Where shining pearle, corall, and many a pounde
On the rich shoare of Amber-Greece is founde
The loftie Cedar which to heaven aspires
The Prince of trees is fewell for their fires
The smoke by which their loaded spitts doe turne
For incense might on sacred Altars burne
Their private roofes on odorous timber borne
Such as might pallaces for Kings adorne
The sweete Palmetta's a new Bacchus yeild
With leaves as ample, as the broadest sheild
Under the shadowe of whose freindly boughs
They sitt carrowsing where their liquor growes
Figgs there unplanted through the feilds doe growe
Such as feirce Cato did the Romans showe
With the rare fruite inviting them to spoyle
Carthage the Mistress of soe rich a soyle
The naked rocks are not unfruitfull there
But att some constant seasons every yeare
Their barren tops wth luscious food abound
And with the Eggs of various fowles are crown'd
Tobacco is their worst of things, which they
To English Landlords, as their tribute pay

Such is the mould that the blest tennant feeds
On pretious fruits, and payes his rent in weeds
With candid Plantines, and the Juicie Pine
On choycest Mellons, and sweete grapes they dine
And with Potatoes fatt their wanton Swine
Nature theis Cates wth such a lavish hand
Powers out among them, that our courser Land
Tasts of that bountie, and doth cloth returne
which not for warmth but ornament is worne
For the kinde Spring, which but salutes vs heere
Inhabites there, and courts them all the yeare
Ripe fruits, and blossoms, on the same trees live
Att once they promise, what att once they give
Soe sweete the ayre, soe moderate the clime
None sickly lives, or dyes before his time
Heaven sure has kept this spott of earth vncurst
To showe how all things were created first
The tardy plants in our cold orchards plac't
Reserve their fruits for the next ages tast
There a small graine in some few moneths wilbee
A firme, a loftie, and a spatious tree
The Palma-Christi, and the faire Papah
Now but a seed (preventing Natures Lawe)
In halfe the Circle of the hastie yeare
Proiect a shade, and lovely fruite doe weare
And as the trees in our dull region sett
But faintly growe, and noe perfection gett
Soe in this Northerne tract our hoarser throats
Vtter vnripe, and ill constreyned notes
Where the supporter of the Poetts style
Phebus on them eternally does smile
Oh how I long my careles limbs to lay
Vnder a Plantanes shade, and all the day
With amarous ayres my fancie entertaine
Invoake the Muses, and improve my vaine
Noe passion there in my free breast should move
None, but the sweete, and best of passions, Love.

here while I sing, if gentle Love bee by)
hat tunes my Lute, and windes the strings soe high)
with the sweete sounde of Sacharissas name
le make the listning Salvadges growe tame
But while I doe these pleasing dreams indite
I am diverted from the promis'd fight.

Canto: 2:

Of their affright, and how their foes
Discovered were, this Canto showes

hough rocks soe high about this Island rise
hat well they may the numerous Turke despise
et is noe humane state exempt from feare
which shakes their hearts, while through the Isle they heare
lasting noyse, as horrid, and as lowd
s thunder makes before it breake the Clowd.
hree dayes they dread this murmure ere they knowe
from what blinde cause th'unwonted sound may growe
t length two Monsters of unequall size
ard by the Shoare, a fisherman espies
woe mighty Whales, which swelling Seas had tost
nd left them prisoners on the rockie Coast
ne as a mountaine vast, and with her came
Cubb, not much inferiour to his Dam
ere in a Poole among the rocks ingag'd
They roar'd like lyons caught in toyles, and rag'd
The man knew what they were, who heeretofore
Had seene the like lye murther'd on the shoare
By the wilde furie of some tempest cast
The fate of shipps, and shipwrackt men to taste
As careles Dames whome wine and sleepe betray
To frantick dreames their infants overlay)
Soe there sometimes the raging Ocean failes
And her owne Brood exposes. when the Whales
Against sharpe rocks like reeling vessells quash't
Though huge as mountaines, are in peeces dasht

Along the Shoare their dreadfull Limbs lye scatter'd
Like hills wth Earthquakes shaken torne and shatter'd
Hearts sure of brass they had whoe tempted first
Rude Seas that spare not, what themselves have nurst.
The welcome news through all the Nation spread
To suddaine ioy, and hope converts their Dread.
What lately was their publique terrour, they
Behold with glad eyes, as a certaine prey
Dispose alreadie of th'untaken spoyle
And as the purchase of their future toyle
These share the bones, and they devide the oyle
Soe was the Huntsman by the Beare oppresst
Whose hide hee sold before he caught the beast.
They man their boates, and all their young men armo
With whatsoever may the monsters harme
Pikes, halberts, spitts, and darts that wound soe faro
The tooles of peace, and instruments of Warr
Now was the time for vigorous Lads to showe
What Love or honour could invite them too
A goodly Theater where rocks are round
With reverent age, and lovely lasses crown'd
Such was the Lake, which held this dreadfull paire
Within the bounds of noble Warwicks share
Warwicks bold Earle then which noe title beares
A greater sound amongst our Brittish Peeres
And worthy hee the memory to renewe
The state and honour to that Title due,
Whose brave adventures have transferr'd his name
And through the new world spread his growing fam
But how they fought, and what their valour gayn
Shall in another Canto bee contain'd. /

Canto: 3:

The bloody Fight, succesles toyle
And how the fishes sack'd the Isle.

The Boate wch on the first assault did goe
Stroke with a harping Iron, the younger foe
Whoe when hee felt his side soe rudely goar'd
Lowde as the Sea that nourish'd him, hee roar'd
As a broad Breame to please some curious tast
While yet alive in boyling water cast
Vext with unwonted heate, bounds, flings about
The scortching brass, and hurles the liquor out
Soe with the barbed Javeling stung, hee raves
And scourges with his tayle the suffring waves
Like fayrie Talus with his Iron flayle
Hee threatnes ruyne with his ponderous tayle
Dissolving att one stroake the battered boate
And downe the men fall drenched in the moate
With every fierce encounter they are forc't
To quitt their boates, and fare like men unhorst.

The bigger Whale like some huge Carracke lay
Which wanteth Sea-roome with her foes to play
Slowly shee swims, and when provoak'd shee would
Advance her tayle, her head salutes the mudd,
The shallowe water doth her force infringe
And renders vaine her tayles impetuous swinge
The shining steele her tender sides receave
And there like Bees they all their weapons leave

This sees the Cubb, and does himselfe oppose
Betwixt his Cumbred Mother and his foes
With desperate courage hee receives her wounds
And men and boates his active tayle confounds
Their furies joyn'd the Seas with billowes fill
And make a tempest though the winds bee still.

Now would the men with halfe their hoped prey
Bee well content, and wish this Cubb away
Their wish they have, Hee to directe his Dam
Unto the Gapp through which they thither came
Before her swimms, and quitts the Hostile Lake
A prisner there but for his Mothers sake
Shee by the rocks compell'd to stay behinde
Is by the vastnes of her bulke confin'd,
They shoute for ioy, and now on her alone
Their furie falls, and all their darts are throwne
Their Launces spent, One bolder then the rest
With his broad sword provokes the sluggish beast
Her oylie side devoures both blade and haft
And there his steele the bold Bermudian left
Courage the rest from his example take
And now they change the colour of the Lake
Blood flowes in Rivers from her wounded side
As if they would prevent the tardie tide,
And rayse the fflood to that propitious height
As might convey her from this fatall streight
Shee swims in blood; and blood does spouting throw
To heaven that heaven mens cruelties might knowe
Their fixed Iavelings in her side she weares
And on her backe a grove of pikes appeares
You would have thought had you the monster seene
Thus drest, she had another Island beene,
Roaring she teares the ayre, with such a noyse
(As well resembled the conspiring voyce
Of routed Armies, when the feild is wonn)
To reach the eares of his escaped Sonn,
Hee though a league removed from the foe)
Hasts to her ayde, the pious Troian soe
Neglecting for Creusa's life, his owne
Repeates the danger of the burning towne
The men amazed blush to see the seede
Of Monsters, humane pietie exceede

Well proved this kindnes, what the Grecians sung
That Loves bright mother from the Ocean sprung
Their courage droopes, and hopeles now they wish
For composition with th'unconquered fish
Soe shee their weapons would restore againe
Throw rocks they'd hew her passage to the Mayne,
But how instructed in each others minde
Or what commerce with men can Monsters finde
Not daring to approach their wounded foe
Whome her couragious Younge protected soe,
They charge their muskets, and with hott desire
Of fell revenge, renew the fight with fire
Standing aloofe, with leade they bruise the scales
And teare the flesh of the incensed Whales
But noe successe their fierce endeavour found
Nor this way could they give one fatall wound
Now to their forte they are about to send
For the lowd Engines which their Isle defend
But what those peices fram'd to batter walls
Would have effected on those mightie Whales
Greate Neptune will not have us knowe, whoe sends
A tide soe high, that it releives his freinds
And thus they parted with exchange of harmes
Much blood the Monsters lost, and they their Armes. /

Upon the deathe of my Ladie Rich

May those alreadie curs'd Essexian plaines
Where hastie deathe, and pyning sicknes raignes
Prove all a desert, and none there make stay
But savadge Beasts, or men as wilde as they
There the faire light, which all our Island grac'd
Like Heros taper in the window plac'd
Such fate from the malignant ayre did finde
As that exposed ~~from~~ to the boistrous winde. /

Ah cruell Heaven to snatch soe soone away
Her for whose life had wee had time to pray
With thousand teares, and vows wee should have sought
That sad decree's suspension to have wrought
But wee (alas) noe whisper of her paine
Heard, till twas time to wish her heere againe
That horrid word at once, like lightning spread
Strooke all our eares The Ladie Rich is Dead
Heart rending newes, and dreadfull to those few
Who her resemble, and her steps pursue
That death should silence have to rage among
The fayre, the wise, the vertuous and the young
The Paphian Queene from that feirce battaile borne
With goared hand, and veyle soe rudely torne
Like terrour did among th'immortalls breed
Taught by her wound, that Goddesses might bleede
All stand amazed, but beyond the rest
Th'Heroique Dame whose happie wombe she blest
Mov'd with iust greife, expostulates with heaven
Vrging that promise to th'obsequious given
Of longer life, for nere was pious soule
More apt t'obey, more worthy to controule
A skilfull eye att once might reade the race
Of Caledonian Monarchs in her face
And sweete humilitie, her looke, and mind
Att once were loftie, and att once were kind.
There dwelt the scorne of vice, and pittie too
For those that did, what she disdaind to doe
Soe gentle, and severe, that what was bad
Att once her hatred, and her pardon had.
Gratious to all, but where her love was due
Soe fast, soe faithfull, loyall, and soe true
That a bold hand as soone might hope to force
The rowling lights of Heaven, as change her course./
Some happie Angell that beholds her there
Instruct vs to record what she was heere
And when this cloude of sorrow's overblowne
Through the wide world, wee'le make her graces knowne.

oo fresh the wound is, and the greife soe vast
hat all our art, and power of speech, is wast,
ere passion swaies, but there the Muse shall rayse
eternall monuments of lowder prayse.
There, our delight complying with her fame
Shall have occasion to write thy name
Faire Sacharissa, and now only faire
To sacred ffriendship wee'le an Altar reare
Such as the Romans did erect of old
Where on a marble pillar shalbee told
The lovely passion each to other bare
With the resemblance of that matchles payre,
Narcissus to the thing, for which he pin'd
Was not more like then yours to her faire mind;
Save that you grac'd the severall parts of life
A spotless Virgin, and a faultles Wife
Such was the sweete converse 'twixt her and you
As that she holds with her associates now.
How false is hope, and how regardles fate
That such a Love should have soe short a date
ately I saw her sighing parte from thee
las that that the last farwell should bee)
Soe look't Astraea her remove design'd
On those distressed freinds she left behind,
onsent in vertue knitt your hearts soe fast
That still the knott in spight of deathe does last
For as yo:r teares, and sorrowe wounded Soule
Prove well that on yo:r parte this bond is whole
oe all wee knowe of what they doe above
s that they happie are, and that they love
et darke oblivion, and the hollowe grave
ontent themselves our frayler thoughts to have
Well chosen Love is never taught to dye
But with our nobler parte invades the skye
Then greive noe more, that one soe heavenly shap'd
The crooked hand of trembling Age escap'd
Rather since wee behold her not decay
But that she vanish'd soe entire away,

Her wondrous Beawtie, and her goodnes merritt
Wee should suppose that some propitious Spiritt
In that celestiall forme frequented heere
And is not dead but ceases to appeare./

To the Queene Mother upon her Landinge

Greate Queene of Europe, where thy offspring weares
All the choise Diadems, whose Princes are thy Heires
As welcome thou to Sea-girt Brittains shoare
As erst Latona (whoe faire Cinthia bore)
To Delos was, heere finds a Kinge as bright
By thee disclos'd with like encrease of light,
Why was her ioy in Belgia soe confin'd
Or why did you soe much regard the wind,
Scarce could the Ocean (though inrag'd) have tost
Thy Soveraigne Barque, but where the obsequious Coast
Paies tribute to thy bed, Romes conquering hand
More vanquish'd Nations, under her command
Never reduc'd. Glad Berecinthia soe
Among her deathles progenie did goe
A wreath of Towers adorn'd her reverend head.
Mother of all that on Ambrosia fedd
Thy Godlike race must sway the age to come
As shee Olimpus peopled with her wombe
Would those commanders of mankinde obey
Their honour'd parent all pretences lay
Downe att yor: royall feete, compose their Iarres
And on the growing Turke discharge those warrs
The Christian Knights, that sacred tombe should wrest
From Pagan hands, and triumph ore the East
There Englands Prince, and Gallia's Dolphin might
Like young Rinaldo and Tancredo fight
In single combate, by their swords againe
The proud Argantes, and fierce Soldan slaine
Againe might wee their glorious deeds write
And with yor: Thuscan Muse exalt the fight./

Songe

Peace babling Muse
I dare not sing, what you indite
Her eyes refuse
To reade the passion which they write
She strikes my Lute, but if it sound
Threatens to hurle it on the ground
And I noe lesse her anger dread
Then the poore wretch that faines him dead
While some feirce Lyon does imbrace
His breathles corps, and licks his face,
Wrapt up in silent feare, hee lyes
Torne all in peices if hee cryes. /

To M:^es Braughton

Faire fellowe Servant, May yo: gentle eare
Prove more propitious to my slighted care
Then the bright Dames wee serve, for her releife
Vext with the long expressions of my greife)
Receive these plaints, nor will her high disdaine
Forbid my humble Muse to court her trayne
Soe in those Nations, which the Sunn adore
Some modest Persian, or some weake eyd Moore
Noe higher dare advance his dazled sight
Then to some guilded Cloude, which neere the light
Of their ascending God adorns the East
And graced with his beames outshines the rest
Thy skilfull hand contributes to our woe
And whetts those arrows which confounds us soe.
A thousand Cupids in those curles doe sitt
Those curious netts your slender fingers knitt,
The Graces put not more exactly on
Th'attire of Venus, when the Ball she woun
Then Sacharissa by thy care is drest
When all our youth prefers her to the rest

You the soft Seasons knowe when best her minde
May bee to pittie or to Love inclyn'd,
In some well chosen houre supply his feare
Whose hopeles Love durst never tempt the Eare
Of that sterne Goddesse, you (her preist) declare
What Offrings may propitiate the ffaire
Rich orient Pearle, bright stones that nere decay
Or polish'd lines which longer last then they:
ffor if I thought she tooke delight in those
To where the cheerfull morne does first disclose,
(The shadie night removing with her beames)
Wing'd with bold Love Ide fly to fetch such Gemms
But since her eyes, her teeth, her lipp excells
All that is founde in mynes, or fishes shells,
Her nobler parte as farre exceeding those
None but Immortall guifts her minde can please
Those shining Jewells Greece and Troy bestow'd
The snowy wrists, and lovely necke did loade
Of Spartas Queene; but when the towne was burn'd
Those fading glories were to Ashes turn'd
Her beautie too had perrish'd, and her fame
Had not the Muse redeem'd them from the fflame. /

To Phillis

Phillis twas Love that iniur'd you
And on that rocke yor Thirsis threw
Whoe for proud Celia could have dy'd
Whilst you noe less accus'd his pride
ffond Love his darts att randome throwes
And nothing springs from what he sowes,
ffrom ffoes discharg'd, as often meete
The shining points of arrowes fleete
In the wide ayre creating fire
As soules that ioyne in one desire
Love made the lovely Venus burne
In vaine, and for the cold youth mourne
Whoe the pursuite of churlish Beasts
Preferd to sleeping on her breasts,

Love makes soe many hearts the Prize
Of the bright Carlisle's conquering eyes
Which she regards not more then they
The teares of lesser beauties weigh.
Soe have I seene the lost clouds powre
Into the Sea a useles Showre
And the vext Saylers curse the raine
For which poore Shepheards curst in vaine.

Then Phillis since our passions are
Governd by chance, and not the care
But sport of heaven, which takes delight
To looke upon this Parthian fight
Of Love, still flying or in chase
Never incountring face to face
Noe more to Love weele sacrifice
But to the best of Deities
And let our hearts, which Love disjoynd
By his kinde mother bee combynd./

Fabula Phœbi et Daphnis./

cradie Iuvenis Thirsis Phœbique Sacerdos
gonti frustra Galateæ ardebat amore
und Deus ipse olim Daphni maiora canebat
er fuit asperior Daphne, nec pulchrior illa
rminibus Phœbo dignis premit ille fugacem
r rupes, per saxa volans, per florida vates
ascua, formosam nunc his componere Nimpham
unc illis crudelem insana mente solebat
idijt illa procul miserum Citharamque sonantem
dijt at nullis respexit mota querelis
e tamen omnino caneret desertus, ad alta
idera perculsi referunt nova carmina montes
it non quæsitis cumulatus laudibus olim
lapsa, reperit Daphni sua laurea Phœbus./

To Amorett

Amorett, the milkie way
Framd of many namelesse starrs,
The smooth streame where none can say
Hee this drop to that prefers.

Amorett my lovely ffoe
Tell mee where thy strength does lye
Where the power that charmes us soe
In thy Soule or in thy eye.

By that snowie necke alone
Or thy grace in motion seene
Noe such wonders could bee done
Yet thy wast is straight and cleane
As Cupids shaft or Hermes rod
And powerfull too as either God./

To my Lord of ffalkland

Brave Holland leads, and with him ffalkland goes
Who heares this told, and does not straight suppose
Wee send the Graces, and the Muses forth
To civilise, and to instruct the North

Not that theis ornaments make swords lesse sharpe
Apollo weares aswell his Bowe as Harpe
And though hee bee the Patron of that Spring
Where in calme peace the sacred Virgins sing,
Hee courage had to guard th'invaded throne
Of Jove, and cast th'ambitious Gyants downe

Ah (noble ffriend) with what impatience all
That knowe thy worth, and knowe how prodigall
Of thy greate Soule thou art, longing to twist
Bayes with that Ivy, which soe early kist
Thy youthfull Temples, with what horrour wee
Thinke on the blind events of Warr and thee
To fate exposing that all knowing breast
Among the throng, as cheaply as the rest

Where Oakes and Brambles (if the Corse bee burn'd)
Unfounded lye to the same ashes turn'd.
Some happie winde over the Ocean blow
This tempest yet, which frights our Iland soe
Guarded with Shipps, and all the Sea our owne
From heaven this mischeife on our heads are throwne
In a late dreame the Genius of this Land
Amaz'd I sawe like the faire Hebrew stand,
When first shee felt the Twinns beginn to Jarr
And founde her wombe the seate of civill Warr
Inclin'd to whose releife, and with presage
Of better ffortune for the present age
Heaven sends, quoth I, this discord for our good
To warme perhapps, but not to waste our blood,
To rayse our drooping Spirits, growne the scorne
Of our proud Neighbours, whoe ere long shall mourne
Though now they Joy in our expected harmes
Wee had occasion to resume our Armes
A Lyon soe, with selfe provoaking smart
His rebell tayle scourging his nobler parte,
Calls upp his courage, then beginns to roare
And charge his ffoes whoe thought him mad before./

Of my Ladie Isabella playing on the Lute./

Such moving sounds from such a carelesse touch
Soe unconcern'd herselfe, and wee soe much?
What Art is this that with soe little paines
Transports us thus, and ore the spirit raignes
The trembling strings about her fingers crowd
And tell their Joy for every kiss aloud
Small force there needs, to make them tremble soe
Touch'd by that hand, whoe would not tremble too?
Heere Love takes stand, and while she charmes the eare
Empties his quiver, on the listning Deere
Musicke soe softens, and disarmes the minde
That not one arrowe does resistance finde.

Thus the faire Tyrant celebrates the prize
And acts herselfe the triumph of her eyes
Soe Nero once, with harpe in hand surveyd
His flaming Rome, and as it burn'd, hee playd./

The Fall

See how the willing earth gave way
To take th'impression where shee lay
See how the mould as loath to leave
Soe sweete a burthen, still does cleave
Close to the Nimphs stayn'd garment, heere
The comming Spring would first appeare
And all this place with roses strowe
If busie feete would let them growe
Here Venus smil'd to see blinde Chance
It selfe before her sonne advance
And a faire Image to present
Of what the Boy soe long had meant,
Twas such a chance, as this made all
The world into this order fall
Thus the first Lovers, on the clay
Of which they were composed, lay
Soe in their prime with equall grace
Mett the first patternes of our race
Then blush not (Faire) or on him frowne
Or wonder how you both came downe,
But touch him, and hee'le tremble streight
How could hee then support your weight
How could the youth (alas) but bend
When his whole Heaven upon him leand
If ought by him amiss were done
Twas that hee let you rise soe soone./

C.F.

Of Silvia

Our Sighes are heard. Just Heaven declares
The sence that has of Lovers cares
Shee that soe farre the rest out shin'd
Silvia the fayre, while shee was kind
As if her frownes impair'd her brow
Seemes only not unhansome now
Soe when the skye makes us endure
A storme, it selfe becomes obscure. /
Hence tis, that I conceale my flame
Hiding from Flammas selfe her name
Least shee provoaking heaven should prove
How it rewards neglected Love
Better a thousand such as I
Their greife untold, should pine and dye
Then her bright morning overcast
With sullen clouds should bee defac't. /

The Bud

Lately on yonder swelling Bush
Bigg with many a comeing Rose
This early budd began to blush
And did but halfe it selfe disclose
I pluck'd it though noe better growne
yet now you see, how full tis blowne.
Still as I did the leaves Inspire
With such a purple light they shone
As if they had byn made of fire
And spreading soe would flame anone
All that was meant by Ayre, or Sunn
To the young flower, my breath has done
If our loose breath so much can doe
What may the same Informes of Love
Of purest Love, and musicke too
When Flavia it aspires to move
When that which lifeles Buds persuades
To wax more soft, her youth Invades. /

To a Ladie singing a songe of his Composinge

Chloris your selfe you soe excell
When you vouchsafe to breath my thought
That like a spiritt with this spell
Of my owne teaching I am taught.

That Eagles fate, and mine are one
Which on the shaft that made him dye
Espide a ffeather of his owne
Wherewith he wont to soare soe high)

Had Eccho with soe sweete a grace
Narcissus lowd complaints return'd.
Not for reflection of his face
But of his voyce the Boy had mourn'd.

Att the marriage of the Dwarfes

Designe or chance makes others wive
But nature did this match contrive
Eve might as well have Adam fled
As she deny'd her little Bed
To him, for whome Heaven seem'd to frame
And measure out this only Dame

Thrice happie is that humble paire
Beneath the levell of all care
Over whose heads those arrows fly
Of sad distrust, and Jealousie
Secured in as high extreame
As if the world held none but them.

To him the fairest Nimphs doe showe
Like moving mountains topt with snowe
And every man a Polypheme
Does to his Galatea seeme
None may presume her faith to prove
Hee proffers deathe, that proffers Love
Ah (Chloris) that kind nature thus
ffrom all the world had sever'd us
Creating for our selves us two
As Love has mee, for only you./

Upon Ben: Johnson

Mirror of poetts, mirror of our Age
Which her whole face beholding on thy Stage
Pleas'd and displeas'd with her owne faults, endures
A remedie like those, whome Musicke cures
Thou hast alone those various inclinations
Which Nature gives to Ages, Sexes, Nations
Hast traced with thy all resembling penn
Whatever Custome has impos'd on men
Or ill gott habitts (which distorts them soe
That scarce one brother can the brother knowe)
Is representing to the wondring Eyes
Of all that see, or reade thy Comedies.
Whoe ever in those glasses looke, may finde
The spotts return'd, or graces of the minde
And by the helpe of soe devine an arte
At leasure view, and dress his nobler parte
Narcissus cozned by that flattering Well
And nothing could but of his beautie tell
Had heere discovering the deform'd estate
Of his fond minde preserv'd himselfe with hate
But vertue too as well as vice is clad
In flesh and blood soe well, that Plato had
Beheld, what his high fancie once embrac't
Vertue with colours, speech, and motion grac't
The sundrie postures of thy copious Muse
Whoe would express, a thousand tongues must use
Whose ffate's noe less peculiar then thy Art
ffor as thou couldst all Characters impart
Soe none cann render thine, whoe still escapes
Like Proteus in varietie of shapes
Whoe was, nor this, nor that, but all wee find.
And all wee can Imagine in mankinde./

To Mr: George Sands on his Translation on some parts of the Bible./

How bold a worke attempts that Penn
Which would enrich our vulgar tongue
With the high raptures of those men
Whoe heere with the same spirritt sung
Wherewith they now assist the Quire
Of Angells whoe their Songs admire.

What ever those inspired Soules
Were urged to expresse did shake
The aged deepe, and both the Poles
Their numrous thunder could awake
Dull earth, which does with heaven consent
To all they wrote, and all they meant

Say (sacred Bird) what could bestowe
Courage on thee to soare soe high
Tell mee (brave ffreind) what help'd thee soe
To shake off all mortallitie.
To light this torch thou hast clymb'd higher
Then hee whoe stole celestiall fire./

Chloris and Hylas

Chl: Hilas oh Hilas why sitt wee mute
Now that each bird saluteth the spring
Winde upp the slacknedd strings of thy Lute
Never canst thou want matter to sing
ffor love thy breast does fill with such a fire
That whatsoe're is faire, moves thy desire.
Hil: Sweetest you knowe the sweetest of things
Of various flowers the Bees doe compose
yet noe particuler taste it brings
Of Violett, Woodbine, Pinke, or Rose
Such love the resultance is of all our graces
Which flowe from a thousand severall faces:

Hilas the Birds which chaunt in this Grove
Could wee but knowe the language they use
They would instruct vs better in Love
And reprehend thy inconstant Muse
For love their breasts does fill with such a fire
That what they once doe choose, bounds their desire

Chloris this change the Birds doe approve
Which the warme Season hither does bring
Time from yo.r selfe does further remove
You, from the winter then the gay Spring
Shee that like lightning shind, while her face lasted
The Oake now resembles which lightning has blasted.

Under a Ladies Picture

Such Hellen was, and whoe cann blame the Boy
That in soe bright a flame consum'd his Troy
But had like vertue shind in that faire Greeke
The amarous Shepheard had not dar'd to seeke
Or hope for pittie, but with silent moane
And better fate had perished alone./

In answer to S.r John Sucklings Verses

Con:

Stay heere fond youth, and aske noe more, bee wise
Knowing too much long since lost Paradise:

Pro:

And by yo.r knowledge wee should bee bereft
Of all that Paradise which yet is left

Con:

The vertuous ioyes thou hast, thou wouldst, should still
Last in their pride, and wouldst not take it ill,
If rudely from sweete dreames, and for a toy
Thou wert awak't, hee wakes himselfe that does Enioy:

Pro:

How can the boy, or hope which you allow
Bee stiled vertuous, and the end not soe
Talke in yor sleepe, and shadowes still admire
Tis true hee wakes that feeles this reall fire
But to sleepe better, for whoe ere drinks deepe
Of this Nepenthe rocks himselfe a sleepe:/

Con:

Fruition adds noe new wealth but destroyes
And while it pleaseth much, yet still it cloyes
Whoe thinks hee shall bee happier made for that
As reasonably might hope, hee might growe fatt
By eating to a surfeit, this once past
What rellishes? even kisses loose their tast./

Pro:

Blessings may bee repeated, while they cloy
But shall wee starve, cause surfeitings destroy;
And if fruition did the taste impaire
Of kisses, why should yonder happie paire
Whose ioyes iust Hymen, warrants all the night
Consume the day too in this less delight?

Con:

Urge not, tis necessarie, alas wee knowe
The homelyest thing that mankinde does is soe
The world is of a large extent wee see
And must bee peopled; Children there must bee
Soe must bread too, but since there are enough
Borne to that drudgerie, What neede wee plough.

Pro

I neede not plough, since what the stooping Hyne
Getts of my pregnant Land, must all bee mine
But in this nobler Tillage tis not soe
For when Anchises did faire Venus knowe
What interest had poore Vulcan in the boy
Greate bold Eneas, or the present Joy.

Con:

Woemen enioy'd what ere before they have beene
Are like Romances read, or Scenes once seene
Fruition dulls, or spoyles the play much more
Then if one read or knew the Plott before.

Pro:

Playes and Romances read and seene doe fall
In our opinions, yet not seene att all
Whome would they please? to an Heroicke tale
Would you not listen, least it should growe stale.

Con:

Tis expectation makes a blessing deare
Heaven were not Heaven, if wee knew what it were./

Pro:

If twere not heaven, if wee knew what it were
Twould not bee heaven to them that now are there./

Con:

As in prospects wee are there pleased most
Where something keepes the eye from being lost
And leaves roome to guess, soe heere restraynt
Holds upp delight that with excess would faynt./

Pro:

Restraynt preserves the pleasure wee have gott
But hee nere has it, that enioyes it not
In goodly prospects who contracts the space
Or takes not all the bountie of the place?
Wee wish remov'd what standeth in our light
And Nature blame for limiting our sight,
Where you stand wisely, winking that the view
Of the faire prospect may bee alwaies new.

Con:

They who knowe all the wealth they have are poore
Hee's only rich that cannott tell his store

Pro:

Not hee that knowes the wealth he has is poore
But hee that dares not touch, nor use his store./

To A: H: of the different success of their Loves./

Thrice happie payre of whome wee cannott knowe
Which first begann to Love, or Loves most now
Faire course of passion, where two Lovers start
And runn togeather hearte still yoakte in hearte
Successfull youth, whome Love has taught the way
To bee victorious in thy first Essay
Sure Loves an Art, best practised att first
And where th'experienc'd still prosper worst
I with a different state pursu'd in vaine
The haughtie Celia, till my iust disdaine
Of her neglect above that passion borne
Did Pride to pride oppose, and scorne to scorne
Now shee relents but all too late to move
A hearte diverted to a nobler Love
The scales are turn'd, her kingdome weighs not more
Now, then my vowes, and service did before:
Soe in some well wrought hangings you may see
How Hector leads, and how the Grecians fly
Heere the fierce Mars his courage soe inspires
That with bold hands the Argive Fleete hee fires
But there from Heaven the blew eyd Virgin falls
And frighted Troy retires within her Walls
They that are formost in that bloodie race
Turne head anon, and give the Conquerours chase
Soe like the chances are of Love and warr
That they alone in this distinguish'd are
In Love the Victors from the vanquish'd fly
They fly that wound, and they pursue that dye./

An Apologie for having lov'd before./

They that never had the use
Of the grapes surprising juyce
To the first delicious cupp
All their reason render upp
Neither doe nor care to knowe
Whether it bee the best or noe./

For they that are to Love inclynde
Sway'd by chance, not Choyce or art
To the first that's fayre or kinde
Make a present of their hearte
'Tis not shee that first wee love
But whome dying wee approve./

To man that was i'th' Evening made
Starrs gave the first delight:
Admiring in the gloomie shade
Those little drops of light
Then att Aurora, whose faire hand
Removed him from the Skyes
Hee gazing towards the East did stand
Shee intertayned his Eyes
But when the bright Sunn did appeare
All those hee gann despise
His wonder was determin'd there
Hee could noe higher rise
Hee neither might, or wish'd to knowe
A more refulgent light
For that as mine your beautye's now
Imploy his utmost Sight./

Palamede to Zelinde
Ariana: Lib: 6:

Fairest Peice of well form'd earth
Urge not thus your haughtie Birth,
The Power wch you have ore us lyes
Not in yor Race, but in yor Eyes,
None but a Prince: alas that voice
Confines you to a narrowe choyce
Should you noe honie vow to tast
But what the Master-Bees have plac't
In compass of their Cells, how small
A portion to yor share would fall
Nor all appeare among those few
Worthy the Stocke from whence they grew
The Sapp wch att the roote is ~~spread~~ bred
In trees, through all the boughes is spread;

But vertues which in parents shine
Make not like progress through the lyne
Tis not from whome, but where wee live
The place does oft those Graces give,
Greate Julius on the mountaines bred.
A flocke perhaps, or heard had led.
Hee that the world subdu'd had been
But the best wrestler on the Greene
Tis Art, and knowledge, which draw forth
The hidden seeds of Native worth
They blowe those sparks, and make them rise
Into such flames, as touch the skyes,
To the old Heroes hence was given
A pedegree which reach'd to heaven
Of mortall seede they were not held.
Which other mortalls soe excell'd:
And beautie too in such excess
As yours, ZELINDE, claymes noe less;
Smile but on mee, and you shall scorne,
Henceforth to bee of Princes borne,
I can describe the shadie Grove
Where your lov'd mother slept with Jove,
And yet excuse the faultles Dame
Caught with her spouses shape, and name
Thy matchles forme will credit bring
To all the wonders I shall sing.